GREAT NORTHERN RAILWAY

Front cover. Northern Bridge Arrival *(Painting by Alan Halfpenny)*

Rear cover. Skegby station *(Painting in author collection)*

Title page: Class O4/1 No. 63602 hits the points at Kirkby South Junction bringing coal from one of the Leen Valley Extension line collieries including some nice cobbles followed by wagons filled with slack.
(Frank Ashley)

by
Bill Taylor

THE LEEN VALLEY EXTENSION

CHAPTERS

ACKNOWLEDGMENTS

As author I would like to acknowledge the advice and assistance I have received in the research and preparation of this book from the following:

The National Archives at Kew for producing various items on my visits including correspondence from Great Northern Railways items in RAIL 226, as well as the very large 2 chain to the inch lithograph plans.

The library staff at Kirkby-in-Ashfield who provided a suitable O.S. Map.
I extend my humble thanks to all the photographers whose work appears in the following pages, grateful that they visited a line which some may regard as a backwater.

For the loan of photographs I am indebted to Richard Morton, Syd Hancock, David Pearce and Robin Cullup who each filled gaps in my material the better to illustrate the text. Gentlemen I thank you all.

I have tried to avoid errors but I must accept personal responsibility for what I have written should any be discovered.

INTRODUCTION

So called because it was a continuation of the line construced by the Great Northern Railway from the outskirts of Nottingham up the valley of the River Leen to tap the lucrative traffic offered by no less than ten coal mines as far north as Newstead. That line was carrying traffic from October 1881 but, further to the north, beyond the high ground known as Robin Hood hills, several new deep mines were being sunk and the GNR saw what today would be called a "business case" to reach thoses mines three of which were being developed by the Stanton Ironworks Company but served only by the rails of the Midland Railway. In the final years of the eighteenth century the new line, christened the Leen Valley Extension in official papers, was opened in stages at a time when railway politics between rival companies was volatile one moment and (fairly) cordial the next. It was at a period when the GNR blocked the Manchester, Sheffield & Lincolnshire Company (Later to change its name to the Great Central Railway) from using the Leen Valley line as part of an intended scheme aimed at reaching London, yet, instead of boring a third tunnel north of Annesley, that company allowed the GNR to share its Annesley tunnel. The Extension line had only been operating for a few years when the two companies realised that their intrests often co-incided with each other, so the politics turned towards rationalisation and even possible merger.

The Leen Valley Extension was about ten miles long and ran from Kirkby South Junction, just north of the high ground referred to by way of Sutton-in-Ashfield, Skegby, Pleasley and Shirebrook before joining what then was the Lancashire, Derbyshire & East Coast Railway. later to be taken over by the GCR to the annoyance of the hesistant GNR, at Langwith Junction. Built primarily for the movement of coal, many thousands of tons of which passed along its rails, there was nevertheless a passenger service until 1931, and then, somewhat surprisingly, again briefly in the BR era. The LNER used it as a diversionary route between Sheffield and Annesley but the end came in 1968, or nearly so. The alignment from Kirky South Junction as far as Summit colliery now forms part of the so called Robin Hood line providing an hourly passenger service between Nottingham and Workop.

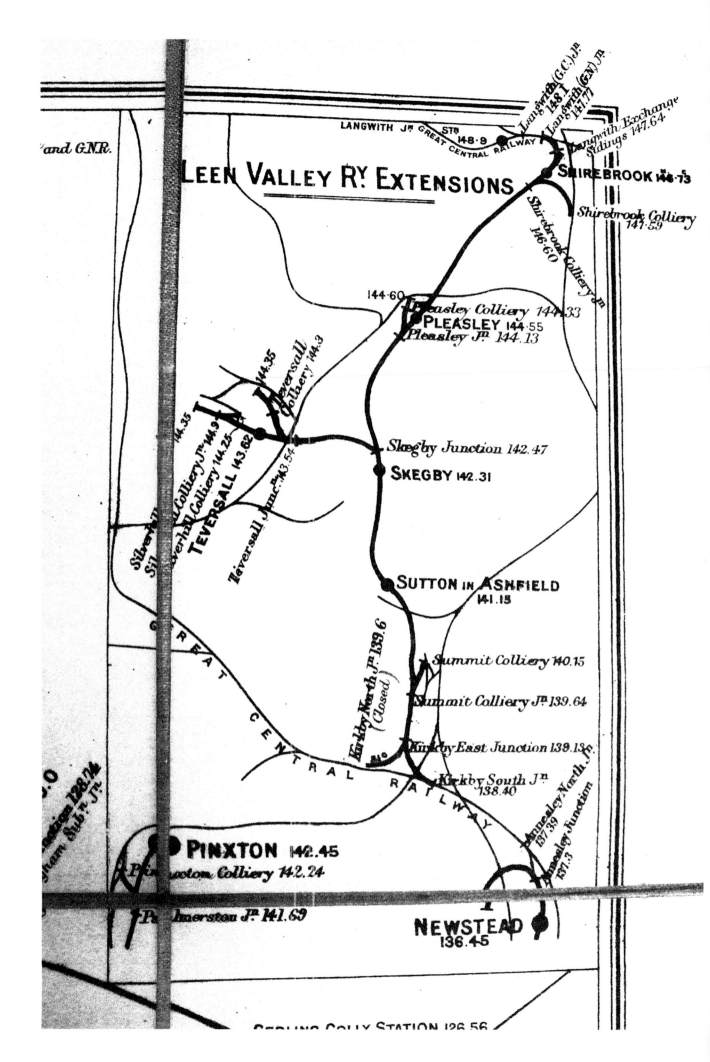

LEEN VALLEY R.Y EXTENSIONS

Langwith (G.C.) J.n 148·1
Langwith (G.N.) J.n 147·77
LANGWITH J.n GREAT CENTRAL RAILWAY STN 148·9
Langwith Exchange Sidings 147·64
SHIREBROOK 146·73
Shirebrook Colliery 147·59
Shirebrook Colliery J.n 146·60
and G.N.R.

144·60
Pleasley Colliery 144·33
PLEASLEY 144·55
Pleasley J.n 144·13

144·35
Teversall Colliery 144·3

Skegby Junction 142·47
SKEGBY 142·31

Silverhill Colliery J.n 144·9
Silverhill Colliery 144·75
TEVERSALL 143·62
Teversall J.n 143·54

SUTTON in ASHFIELD 141·15

Kirkby North J.n 139·6 (Closed)
Summit Colliery 140·15
Summit Colliery J.n 139·64

Kirkby East Junction 139·13

GREAT CENTRAL RAILWAY

Kirkby South J.n 138·40
Annesley North J.n 137·39
Annesley Junction 137·3

...tions 128·74
...ham Sub. J.n.

PINXTON 142·45
Pinxton Colliery 142·24

Palmerston J.n 141·69

NEWSTEAD 136·45

GEDLING COLLY STATION 126·56

4

THE LEEN VALLEY EXTENSION LINE OF THE GREAT NORTHERN RAILWAY

"There is no better example of how Victorian railway politics worked than this sudden rash of new lines around Kirkby-in-Ashfield and Sutton-in-Ashfield" M.A.Vanns.

SETTING THE SCENE.

In the above quotation Michael Vanns is referring to the promotion and development of new railways in the years from 1888 to the end of the 19th century. Three pre-grouping companies constructed lines in the area referred to; these were the Midland Railway (MR) established by the merger of three smaller concerns in 1844 based at Derby, the Great Northern Railway (GNR) whose system included the East Coast main line from Kings Cross to beyond Doncaster with a strong presence in Lincolnshire and the West Riding of Yorkshire, and finally the Manchester Sheffield & Lincolnshire Railway (MS&L) whose territory is obvious from its title but who harboured a desire to expand southwards from Sheffield to Nottingham and eventually to London.

The epicentre of the MR was arguably Trent from which station lines radiated in all directions rather like the spokes of a wheel. Because it expanded in the early years of railway construction not only did it secure a monopoly in many towns which went unchallenged for thirty years, it also obtained the most favourable routes from an engineering standpoint, often following valleys thereby keeping construction costs relatively low. By the 1850s it owned routes between Nottingham and Derby, the line from Trent up the Erewash valley and on to Clay Cross where it joint the direct line from Derby to the north, as well as the branch from Nottingham shadowing the River Leen via Annesley heading to Mansfield. These lines together with the established route north of Chesterfield generated much revenue to the company from goods and mineral traffic originating at factories, ironworks and coal mines located close to them. The MR had the field to themselves.

The GNR looked enviously to the west of its main line but in 1860 all it had in the East Midlands was the line from Grantham to Nottingham which in the earlier years one Mr. Hutchinson had somehow managed to keep from falling into Derby's expanding empire. It owned the attractive station on London Road, more than adequate for the few passenger trains using its Nottingham terminus, but transporting goods made in the city's factories yielded a modest income. At that time the GNR did receive coal from the MR, a little handed to it in Nottingham but more at Hitchin thus producing income on a mileage basis, though the company was not directly connected to a colliery in the region. With the arrival of the MR at St. Pancras nearly all of that revenue was lost over night.

Kings Cross looked again at its presence in Nottingham and the Directors decided it would need to spend a good deal of capital (which it would have to raise) if it were to secure a decent share in the profitable business of taking coal away from the expanding Notts/Derbyshire coalfield. A line was planned to leave the Nottingham branch just to the west of the River Trent crossing, looping round the northern outskirts of the city before heading west to Derby, the very heart of the MR, and then beyond to reach Burton-on-Trent and Stafford with help from the North Staffordshire Railway. A branch line to serve the established mining concerns was thrown off to the north up the Erewash valley to a terminus at Pinxton. These new lines were all busy with GNR trains in 1876 and represented the first serious inroads into what the MR had regarded as its own exclusive territory. Now the coal owners could choose which company to use to get their product away and that brought down the cost of transport. The country needed coal both for domestic and industrial use, as well as for ships of the Royal Navy and the merchant fleets, to say nothing of the quantities used by the railway companies themselves. In addition there was a lively export trade in the "black gold". To meet these demands more mines were sunk, usually to the east of those already in production or close to being worked out, and now it was the turn of the Leen valley to see colliery headstocks rising from the ground. The GNR had shown the Derbyshire mine owners what they could do, so now they would be welcomed to Bestwood, Hucknall, Linby and Newstead to compete with the haulage rates per ton per mile levied by Derby. By 1882 GNR trains had reached Newstead just south of the ridge of high ground near Annesley known as the Robin Hood Hills. There it would rest for a while.

Next it was the turn of the MS&L, ready and anxious to extend its system. Its Chairman was the redoubtable Edward Watkin (later Sir Edward Watkin) an astute and ambitious, though sometimes crafty and untrusted mover among his equals, a shrewd, often single minded railway promoter and politician, who needed to change his provincial MS&L into the Great Central Railway (GCR) serving the capital. An often neglected aspect of MS&L history both before and after it changed its name to GCR is its involvement in joint lines, the largest, of course, being the Cheshire Lines Company. It was nevertheless a partner in more joint lines than any other pre-grouping railway company. This, it is submitted, is where Watkin's style and approach could be said to be both shrewd and astute, but on one notable occasion he so upset the Directors of the GNR that he was (and deserved to be) rebuked in no uncertain terms. The occasion was in 1871 when a Bill was before parliament for the construction of a new line from Long Stanton to Market Rasen promoted by one Mr. Baxter, but supported by Watkin. The background is rather complicated but suffice it to say that Watkin was looking to have an independent route to get South Yorkshire coal to London and the Eastern counties. In giving evidence to parliament and referring to the GNR, Watkin said *"I cannot trust you, I tell you frankly."* This was outrageous especially when the GNR had given good rates for the onward transport of South Yorkshire coal handed to it by the MS&L, and had suffered losses from the Derbyshire traffic as a result. Edmund Denison's response is worth quoting in full.

"I have not invited this issue of the confidence of the Manchester, Sheffield Company or in Sir Edward Watkin personally; but if Sir Edward Watkin choses to come here and tell a body of gentlemen such as the Great Northern Board that he cannot trust them, he invites inquiry into his own antecedents. I am merely dealing with him in his railway character – in any other character I have nothing to say to him – but I should like to know if any Company in England has done such things as the Manchester, Sheffield have done – hawked itself about as buyer, as seller, as guarantor and guarantee; bribed to shut up their traffic, bribed to open their traffic. There is not a conceivable bargain to which they have not been parties, and here they come to ask to have justice. I only wish it to be administered to them."

Returning to 1888 the MS&L lines came no further south than a junction with the MR at Beighton, to the south-east of Sheffield. The first move into the area which this book deals with came with the Act authorising the so-called Derbyshire Lines piercing the Robin Hood ridge to make an end on connection with the GNR Leen Valley metals at Annesley. This might have given the MS&L access to Nottingham but the GNR Directors saw through his plan fearing that the line would be used as part of a further route to the South. To allow Watkin running powers from Annesley to Nottingham without restriction would give him a clear road to promote a line from there to London and would be disastrous. No surprise, therefore, that any proposal while Watkin was at the helm of the MS&L would be viewed with great suspicion.

Before looking closely at the politics, proposals and events of the period closely concerned with the Leen Valley extension route we should not forget that there was a fourth major company anxious to have a share of the lucrative coal traffic, and that was the London & North Western Railway (LNWR). The policy they adopted was quite different but, being powerful in the land and with many friends in parliament able to influence decisions, they built no new lines in the district. Granted they had their own locomotive depot at Colwick and a separate goods depot in Nottingham at Manvers Street, but neither of these involved substantial outlay of capital. Instead they petitioned against virtually every new railway which was proposed to be built, then, in exchange for running powers over the proposed lines, their objections were withdrawn.

Being private undertakings railway companies needed to secure the consent of both Houses of Parliament to secure the necessary Act in order to construct a new line, and this required detailed plans and books of reference to be printed and lodged with Clerks of the Peace for all the areas through which the proposed line would pass and also deposited with parliament no later than the 30th November prior to the year when the Bill was considered. In 1888 the MS&L made no secret of the fact that it would seek powers in the next session to construct a line from Beighton via Staveley and Tibshelf to join the existing GNR metals at Annesley, a line which would open up the area through which it passed and be of benefit to the manufacturing and other businesses within easy reach of its route. At first glance the proposal seemed reasonable enough, filling a gap where the MR had no competition and seeking running powers to Nottingham for passenger and general goods traffic in exchange for which the GNR would be allowed to run its own trains along the whole of the proposed line and even to Sheffield. Sir Henry Oakley, the GNR Chairman stood firm and stipulated that access to Nottingham was not to be used in order to facilitate a later southward extension. An undertaking to that effect was sought but the MS&L refused to give it, a clear sign of its ultimate intentions.

The session of 1889 included two railway Bills before Parliament affecting the localities of Kirkby-in-Ashfield and Sutton-in-Ashfield. As expected the MS&L Derbyshire Lines scheme was there but in addition the MR put forward a west to east line passing through Sutton-in-Ashfield, which would have included a station much closer to the town centre. The GNR petitioned against the MS&L scheme in the Commons urging that no further extension south of Nottingham should be allowed as it would breach the terms of a Fifty Year Agreement between them dated 1860. Despite this the Bill passed to the Lords where a further attempt was made to defeat it. Eventually the MS&L in order to secure its Act conceded that running powers to Nottingham over the GNR would only be used for access to that city asserting it had no plans to go further, but saying that the use of the proposed line would be entirely under its own control. In effect if a further push south were to happen it would have to start at Annesley. The MS&L got its Derbyshire Lines Act and the GNR started to make plans to protect its investment in the Leen valley.

The following year was one of reflection and planning for the railway companies involved. The MR took a second look at its east to west line and chose to abandon it in favour of affording the residents of Sutton-in-Ashfield a more conveniently located station on High Pavement by means of a short branch from Sutton Junction. They had realised that the GNR was minded to promote a line from its existing terminus at Annesley which would pass through the centre of town where a most conveniently located station would be provided on Outram Street.

Neither the MS&L nor the GNR advanced a local Bill in 1890 but, behind the scenes much was happening. The MS&L was getting on with its Beighton to Annesley line whilst still harbouring a desire to reach London. The coalfield was expanding with new and deeper mines being proposed and sunk a little to the east of the older pits some of which were being worked out. The GNR had lost some of its mineral traffic as previously mentioned and also as a result of further disagreement with the MR, and it feared further contraction if eventually the MS&L took its own coal south of Nottingham. It was therefore anxious to tap into as many sources of new business as possible so looked closely at likely development near to the Notts/Derbyshire border between Annesley and Langwith, and out of this was born the resolution to seek powers to construct what came to be known as the "Leen Valley Extension" lines. Late in 1890 the MS&L deposited plans to build a line from Annesley to Quainton Road where a junction would be made with the Metropolitan Railway, a very expensive project which would require an

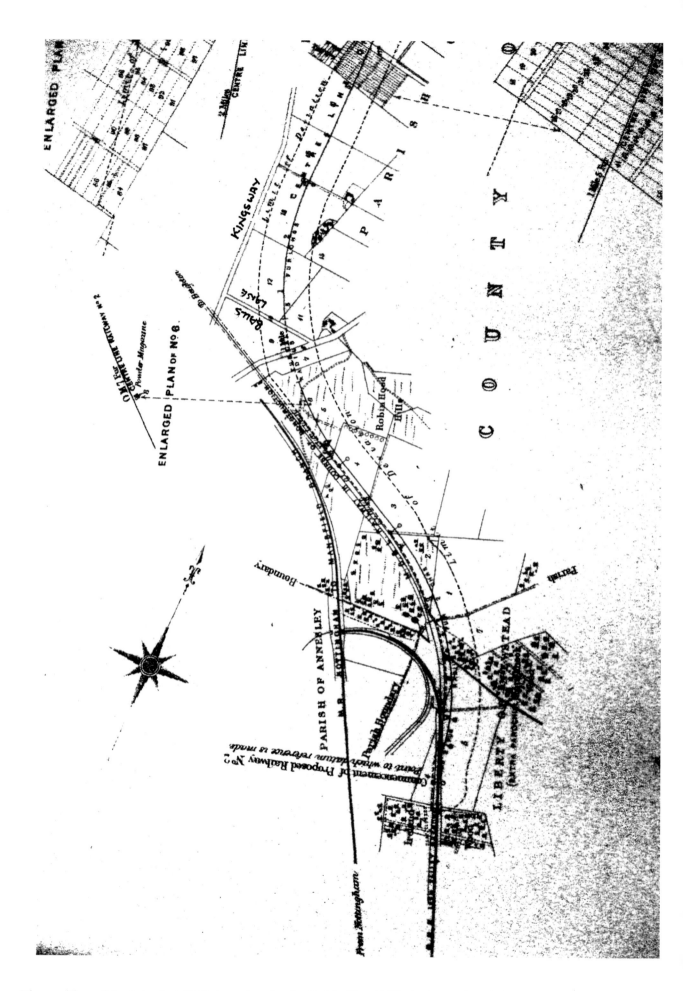

The position of the intended GNR tunnel under the Robin Hood hills is shown in relation to the Midland Railway (MR) line and the MS&L then under construction.

View looking south at Annesley with the MS&L line curving away to join the GNR Leen Valley line beyond the signal in the distance, the connection giving the MS&L access from the north to Nottingham but no further courtesy of running powers. The latter's desire to reach London necessitated starting from Annesley close by the buffer stop destined to become Annesley North Junction. *(Author collection)*

Class B1 No. 61285 wheels a short goods train across Annesley GN Junction. Going off to the left is the former GNR line serving Annesley colliery which appears to be rather busy with empty wagons being pushed towards the mine and another locomotive stood on the departure track. To the right the northern entrance to the former GCR goods yards can be made out at a lower level. The signal passed by the B1 is probably a replacement of the one referred to in the previous photograph. *(David Dykes)*

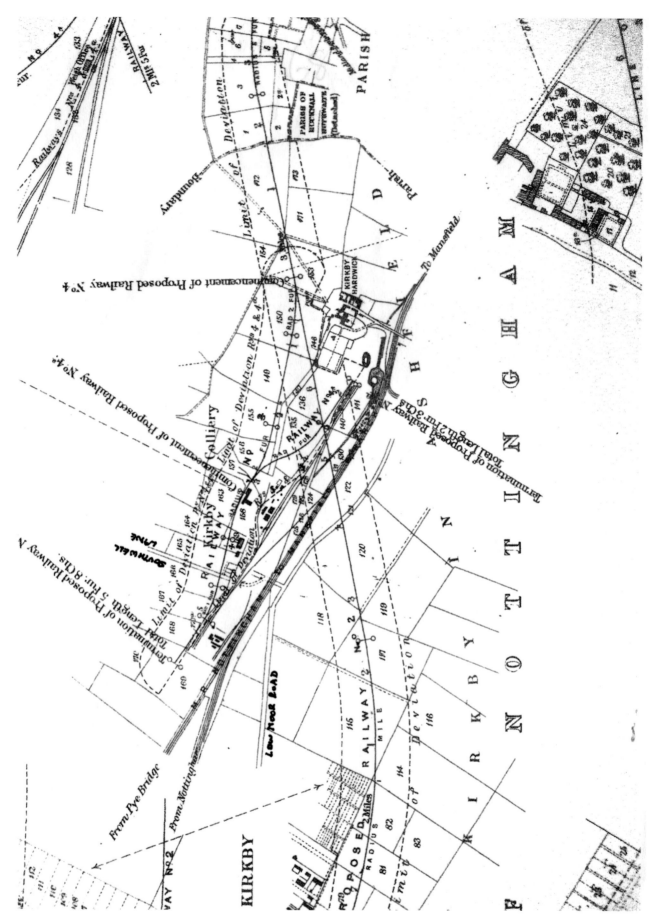

This plan shows the original proposal for the lines serving Summit colliery (shown as Kirkby Colliery on the plan). Had these lines been constructed they would have crossed the MR Nottingham to Mansfield line close by Kirkby Hardwick which today marks the location of Sutton Parkway station on today's Robin Hood line. A reverse connection to serve the colliery on the down side would have resulted in a complicated shunting manoeuvre to bring away the loaded wagons.

enormous amount of capital to be raised. Possibly tongue in cheek it approached the GNR suggesting this new line should be built between them, thus affording the latter a better presence in both Nottingham and Leicester. (They already had a presence in both places.) Still suspicious of Watkin, Sir Henry Oakley wisely declined the idea, preferring instead to draw up detailed plans for his company to close the gap between Annesley and Langwith.

1891 was a very busy year for railway Bills affecting Nottinghamshire in parliament. The MS&L intent on having separate access to the London area was opposed by many other companies who saw their traffic and territory being invaded. The GNR not only petitioned strenuously against that Bill, they also put forward their Bill for the Leen Valley Extension lines. Starting from Annesley the line would have required a third tunnel through the high ground forming the Robin Hood hills. In addition, a newcomer, the Lancashire Derbyshire & East Coast Railway (LDEC) whose grandiose coast to coast line was planned to pass through the Langwith/Shirebrook area used up a great deal of committee time, having been opposed by the Midland, MS&L and Great Northern. The outcome was that the LDEC got its Act causing the furious Watkin, whose Bill failed, to condemn it as "the maddest scheme ever presented to parliament." However, now it had been approved the GNR saw the chance to discuss possible junctions at Langwith, and with the MS&L setback, the pressure was off. The GNR withdraw its Bill but clearly would renew the application the following year.

Various reasons have been suggested by earlier writers as to why the Bill was withdrawn. Birks & Coxon put it down to the demands of other GN business in parliament, while Leleux says it was due to the failure of the MS&L Bill, a view shared by Vanns who noted that it had served its purpose. It had indeed served its purpose, but, noting that construction work on the line did not start till summer 1895 the GNR may have felt it was slightly premature as well.

In 1892 the MR had started to build the short branch to Sutton-in-Ashfield, and the MS&L tried again, this time successfully, to get its London Extension Bill through parliament. The GNR saw that some work had been started by the LDEC east of Chesterfield and, as intended, sought and obtained its Act to construct what would in part be a difficult line from Annesley to Langwith.

Leaving the existing Leen valley branch just south of where the authorised MS&L junction would be located the new line was to run on the eastern side of the MS&L keeping close company with it before veering away to pierce the high ground by a tunnel 270 yards in length passing under what is now Derby Road and emerging on the north side of Balls Lane. Negotiating a curve of five furlongs radius both sides of the tunnel the line then ran straight in a north westerly direction parallel to but to the east of Kingsway before crossing the MR Nottingham to Mansfield line close by Kirkby Hardwick. This section would have passed through what is now Kingsway Cemetery and over Diamond Avenue to the east of the old school. Adjacent to Kirkby Hardwick a short branch line was authorised running south westerly to serve Kirkby Colliery, locally known as Summit pit. The main line turned north again heading towards Sutton-in-Ashfield. None of the above mentioned lines were constructed in the event because relations with the MS&L had improved sufficiently for them to allow the GNR to use its tunnel thus giving birth to Kirkby South Junction as the springboard for the Leen Valley extension lines.

The Act of 28 March 1893 sanctioned the new route which as far as Summit colliery was constructed on an alignment which the present day Robin Hood line follows almost exactly, though in part at significantly different levels. Beyond the colliery the line made towards Sutton-in-Ashfield passing first below the MR branch to that town before reaching Outram Street where the first station would be built. The alignment continued to Skegby, the site of another station and also junction of the branch giving access to two collieries, Teversal and Silverhill. Beyond the junction the main line would be on a falling gradient

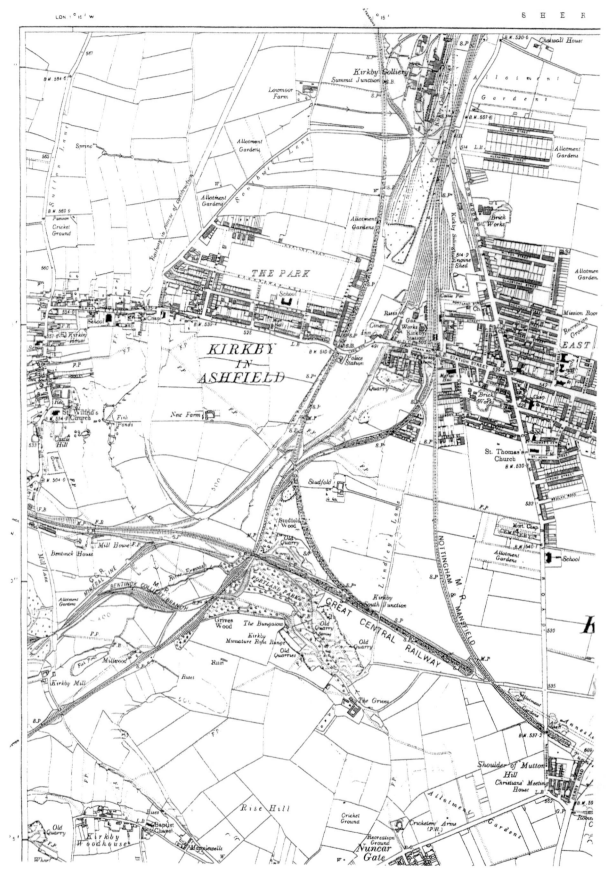

The 1914 edition of the O.S.Map shows the position of all railway lines constructed in the Kirkby area except, of course, the 1972 deviations. Annesley tunnel, Kirkby South Junction and Summit colliery are clearly marked as also is the abandoned curve from a point near to the police station to the GCR line. The Mansfield Railway is shown as in the course of construction severing the abandoned GNR line and will continue to join the GCR at Kirkby South Junction. The present day Robin Hood line emerges from the MR Kirkby tunnel at bottom right then closely follows the GCR alignment passing above Lindleys Lane before taking the Leen Valley Extension formation to Summit signal box at the top of the map.

towards Shirebrook serving Pleasley colliery, where there would also be a station, along the way. Just before Shirebrook station site was reached a short but steep branch line would connect with the coal mine of the same name. The ultimate destination was the coal mine at Langwith but to reach it would require the new lines to cross the LDEC tracks at the very point where that company's Chesterfield and Sheffield routes diverged, namely at Langwith Junction.

Railway No. 2 in the GNR Act veered north west from the termination of the main line at 10 miles and 2 furlongs from Annesley, passing over the LDEC Chesterfield line a short distance west of Langwith Junction to joint that company's Sheffield branch, while railway No. 3 also commenced at the same point as railway No. 2 continuing over the LDEC and the MR Worksop line in a more direct approach to Langwith colliery. It is submitted that these were tactically promoted lines because, as events developed it proved unnecessary to construct either of them when, by agreement between the two railway companies a small portion of Railway No. 3 was built on embankment then realigned to make a junction with the LDEC just east of Langwith Junction station. This junction faced west thus giving direct access to the LDEC Sheffield line, and thereby to Langwith colliery.

Copy of contemporary postcard showing a Stirling locomotive on passenger train at Shirebrook around 1910.
(Author collection)

CONSTRUCTION AND OPENING.

Unlike the position further to the west where the earliest worked coal outcropped at or close to the surface, in the area traversed by the route of the newly authorised railway the coal seams were overlaid by magnesian limestone. The mining companies had to drill through this very hard rock before reaching the top hard coal seam, but they only had to do so vertically, whilst the GNR contractor's task was to drive through it to all intent and purposes horizontally. The building of only ten miles of new line would certainly not be easy, indeed it started straight away in the cutting at Kirkby South Junction. The limestone ridge ran along the boundary separating the west side of Nottinghamshire from Derbyshire causing the navvies to battle with it along much of the way.

Going north the summit of the line was quickly reached in the vicinity of Kirkby Hardwick, the main line then being on a falling gradient almost the entire way to Shirebrook. The branch to Teversal, however, rose sharply for a short distance from Skegby Junction, before levelling out and then falling slightly on the approach to the coal mines. The earlier GNR line up the Leen valley to Annesley climbed all the way from the outskirts of Nottingham facilitating a downhill run for loaded trains towards Colwick Yards. Except for Summit colliery, the output from the mines served by the new line had to be hauled on adverse gradients for the initial few miles.

In one respect the name "Leen Valey Extension" is a misnomer. True the line was an extension of the railway line up the valley of the River Leen, but that river springs from the Robin Hood Hills and flows towards Nottingham. The line which this book deals with starts at Kirkby-in-Ashfield close to the source of the Erewash but swiftly crosses the watershed to where the Maun rises before turning away to follow the Meden valley. During this late period in the development of Britain's railways the promoters were keenly aware of the dislike by municipal bodies of level crossings especially where anything other than an occupation road had to be crossed. The surveyors had been careful in selecting the route and adjusting the gradient where necessary to such a degree that no level crossing was proposed on the new railway. Engineering was heavy for much of the way, especially in relation to cuttings which required to be formed by blasting away significant amounts of magnesian limestone. In some locations the waste had to be taken away, but at Skegby as well as on a portion of the alignment between Pleasley and Shirebrook, it was used nearby to form embankments.

It may seem strange at this distance in time that, despite the plans securing parliamentary approval in June 1893, the GNR was in no hurry to start building the railway, so it was to be all of two years later when construction commenced. The delay cannot be explained by the alterations at the southern end of the line as the use of the MS&L tunnel had been settled in 1893. In his epic work, "The History of the Great Northern Railway", Charles Grinling explains that the company was heavily committed elsewhere at the time and this may go some way to account for the tardiness. The first contract was awarded to Walter Binns of Bradford in 1895 after the Stanton Ironworks Company, proprietors of the coal mines at Teversal, had urged the company to *"get on with the job"*. Shortly before his retirement Richard Johnson M.I.C.E., the chief engineer of the GNR, persuaded the company to construct the line as far as Pleasley colliery, including the Teversal branch, albeit initially as a single line. By doing this the coal produced by four of the six mines intended to be served would be collected thereby starting the flow of a reliable income, at the same time allowing more time to complete what would inevitably be a more difficult section beyond Pleasley. Work started in June 1895 on the deep curved cutting through the hard mineral at the place where the new line parted company with the MS&L to the north of Annesley tunnel. Next the MR Pye Bridge line was bridged before another cutting needed to be carved out in order to reach Summit colliery. Binns was given an advance payment in order to progress the works which, by the following January, were making steady progress. Nevertheless it was to be September before the

QUARRYING THE RED STONE OUT OF THE CUTTING FOR BRIDGE BUILDING.

AT WORK ON THE WINGS : BOTTOM LIFT SHEWING CRANES AT WORK IN THE GULLET IN THE DISTANCE.

Magazine illustrations depicting construction work in deep limestone cuttings on the Leen Valley Extension line.
(Feilden Magazine)

The Stanton Ironworks Co. coal mine at Teversal. The original headstocks and chimneys are prominent in the distance as well as the brickworks on the left. The railway line is part of the pit's internal system. Both Teversal and the nearby Silverhill collieries were served by the GNR and the MR. *(Author collection)*

The GNR line remains in a cutting, though not too deep, at this point as it passes below first the MR Sutton Junction to Sutton-in-Ashfield branch then Station Road seen in the distance. *(GNR official photograph)*

formation reached the mine.

Two branch lines to serve Summit colliery, owned by the Butterley Company, both on the up side of the formation, each 58 chains in length leading respectively to the full and empty wagons roads, were controlled by an adjacent brick built signal box. The expectation was that some 4000 tons of coal each day would be brought to the surface within a few years, so the GNR could anticipate a healthy traffic developing on its lines despite being in competition with the MR, whose metals were adjacent to the shaft but on the opposite side of the colliery site. About a quarter of a mile beyond the colliery branch the summit of the main line was attained, and now, on a falling grade of 1 in 120 the formation entered a shallow cutting which however required 213,000 cubic yards of material to be excavated and a second MR line to be avoided, this time the Sutton-in-Ashfield branch overhead. Some careful preparation was needed here so as to cause the minimum of disruption to that company's traffic. The brick abutments were built in trenches but the ground between them was not removed until the steel girders of the bridge supporting the MR permanent way was built on staging alongside and fully asphalted and ballasted. After the passage of the last MR train on the Saturday night the contractors took possession of the branch line to remove the rails before sliding the new ones into place by using wire ropes and crab winches, thus restoring the formation in time for the first Sunday Midland train to pass. The GNR line then continued the short distance to Sutton-in-Ashfield, where adjacent to the site of the first station along the new line the track was level. Most of the two and a half miles (approx) to this point had been excavated through limestone cuttings but not without difficulty as noted in the Mansfield Advertiser.

"Throughout the whole length the water from the limestone has been a source of great trouble, and the forcing through of cuttings seems to have opened up all the springs in the district."

Sutton-in-Ashfield station was very conveniently located close to the town centre between Outram Street and Priestsic Road, both being carried above the railway by substantial bridges with stone abutments. The station entrance was on Outram Street the level of which was raised on both approaches to avoid the need for a level crossing and sufficient land was acquired for a goods yard to serve the developing town. Beyond Priestsic Road the route passed below Stoneyford Lane prior to entering the Skegby cutting, which was driven through using a Ruston Navvy machine as well as explosives. Emerging from this forty feet deep cutting the line was carried on a short embankment then over the main road by a girder bridge to reach Skegby station whose platforms were at the top of a covered stairway, unlike at Sutton-in-Ashfield where the opposite was the case. In order to accommodate the line Buttery Lane was realigned a little way to the west to form a new junction with the main road, and the Prince of Wales Tree was removed. Skegby Junction marked the point where the single line branch leading to Teversal (also known as Butcherwood) and Silverhill collieries climbed away on the down side, initially on embankment before passing through a shallow cutting to reach the sidings where the loaded wagons would be waiting. The main line continued on a falling gradient past Skegby Junction mainly on embankment formed in part by the material excavated from Skegby cutting, following the River Meden to Pleasley.

In February 1897 the local newspaper reported that the workforce engaged in construction of the line had reduced from almost 900 the previous year to 650 as well as the arrival on 9 February of the first raft of empty coal wagons at Sutton-in-Ashfield, the line having been officially opened the previous day. The section from Kirkby Summit to Teversal was brought into use without ceremony, albeit only as a single line beyond Sutton-in-Ashfield because the contractors retained possession of one set of rails to move the remaining spoil from Skegby cutting to the formation still in hand towards Pleasley, which it was estimated, would take about six months to complete. The pits at Silverhill and Teversal each turned out 2000 tons of coal every working day, so there was enough for two railway companies to share, and in due course Pleasley's daily output of 2500 tons would bring additional revenue to the Leen Valley

Menu of Luncheon.

❖ ❖

SALMON AND CUCUMBER.
LOBSTER SALADS.

❖ ❖

LAMB AND MINT SAUCE. SIRLOIN OF BEEF.
PRESSED BEEF. YORK HAMS. TONGUES.
PIGEON PIES. VEAL PIES.
ROAST AND BOILED CHICKENS.
ROAST DUCKS, APPLE SAUCE.
BONED TURKEYS

❖ ❖

TRIFLES. JELLIES. CREAMS.
STEWED FRUITS. PASTRY.

❖ ❖

CHEESE AND SALAD.

❖ ❖

GRAPES. PINES. APPLES. ORANGES.
DRIED FRUITS. FILBERTS.

❖ ❖

CHAMPAGNE.
CIGARS.

Toast List.

❖ ❖

"THE QUEEN AND ROYAL FAMILY."
HON. REGINALD CAPEL.

———

THE CHAIRMAN TO DECLARE THE
NEW LINE OPEN.

———

"SUCCESS TO THE NEW LINE AND THE
GREAT NORTHERN RAILWAY."
MR. F. J. TURNER.

REPLY—MR. F. W. FISON, M.P.

———

"PROSPERITY TO THE TRADE OF
SUTTON-IN-ASHFIELD AND DISTRICT."
SIR HENRY OAKLEY.

REPLIES—MR. J. C. SAMPSON.
MR. J. A. LONGDEN (STANTON IRON CO.)

The Special Train will leave Sutton-in-Ashfield at about
3.0 p.m. for Nottingham.

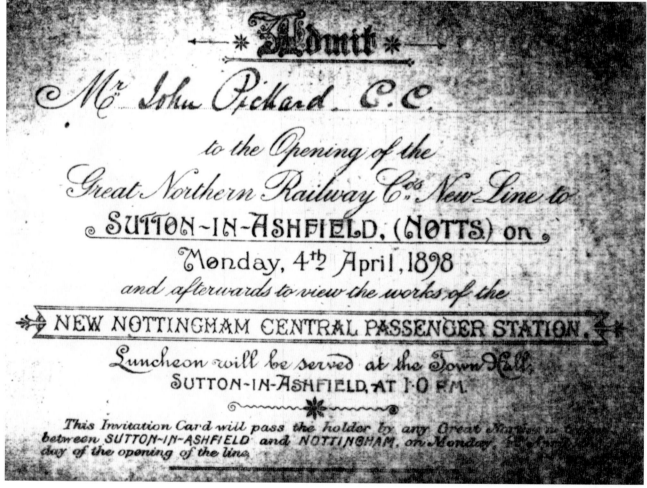

Personal invitation and Menu and Toast List sent to County Councillor Pickard to celebrate the opening of the line to Sutton-in-Ashfield in 1898.

(Sutton Library/ Author collection)

extension lines.

Difficulties encountered in completing the works comprised in his contract proved too much for Walter Binns, who was relieved from his obligations when the Halifax Commercial Banking Company took on the responsibility to complete the remaining works on 7 May 1897. The cutting at Skegby was finished and a double line of railway was laid as far as Pleasley Colliery under their direction, the earlier estimate of about six months to reach that point being too optimistic as it was to be 1March 1898 before that section was sanctioned by the Board of Trade for goods and mineral trains to run.

The Directors must have been well satisfied with the situation because they arranged for the formal opening for all traffic to Sutton-in-Ashfield to be marked with some ceremony. The event included a luncheon in the Town Hall there on 4 April 1898 at one o'clock when invited guests were treated to a five course repast served by Mr. Keeley, licensee of the Denmans Head Hotel, starting with lobster salad, followed by sirloin of beef, veal pie or roast duckling as a main course, then trifle or stewed fruits. For those still hungry cheese and salad was placed on the tables and finally dried fruits and filberts. Mr. A. H. Bonser, the county councillor for the district sent out on 28 March from his office at Forest Lodge almost two hundred invitations to representatives of local industry and commerce requesting a response within two days.

Seated at the top table were Councillor Bonser, Sir Henry Oakley General Manager of the GNR, Mr. Thomas Warner Turner, land and estate agent representing the Duke of Portland, Mr. J. A. Longden of the Stanton Iron Company, The Hon. Reginald Capel Deputy Chairman of the GNR, Mr. R. M. E. W. Dodsley Squire of Skegby, and Aldermen. Other guests were placed on either side of five long tables running at right angles to the top table, each side accommodating eighteen persons. At the far end of each such table a place was laid for a senior member of GN staff and these included Mr. W. J. Grinling Assistant Manager, Mr. H. A. Ivatt, Locomotive Engineer and Mr. Ross the Engineer. The seating plan has survived (RAIL 1016/1) and includes many of the town's well known businessmen, examples being Tudsbury (hosiery), Barringer (Metal Box Co.), Fidler (solicitor), Wass (quarry owner), Briggs (jeweller and pawnbroker), Searson (builder), Buckland (hosiery), Hepworth (outfitter), Willey (butcher), and Hutchinson (furnisher).

The following are extracts from the report in the Notts. Free Press of 8 April 1898:

Luncheon over and the loyal toasts duly honoured the Chairman declared the line open. He remarked how gratified the representatives of the Great Northern Company were to find such a large assembly there. He had had the pleasure of being introduced to and of shaking hands with a few of the company, and he was quite prepared to be introduced to and to shake hands with everybody in the room.(Laughter and applause) He looked upon that good old English custom of shaking hands as a sort of understanding, a sort of unwritten contract, that they would be true to one another. The Great Northern Company looked to the traders of that district to give them as much as they possibly could of their merchandise, and in return the Company would give them punctuality, expeditiousness, and reasonable rates.(Hear, hear) He was quite sure if the Company did not fulfil their part of the contract they would hear of it sooner or later. (Laughter and applause) Now, as they knew, the Company had only been in that town for a very little while, but so far as he could judge – and he was sorry not to have had better opportunities of looking round the place – there appeared to be evidence of great prosperity, immediate and prospective, and the Great Northern Company hoped that the development which would be caused by their railway being extended up north would be of very great assistance to that town and its industries (Applause) They had always heard that Sutton-in-Ashfield was a thriving town, and he did not think they should have spent something like half a million of money unless they had thought it was worth the while to do so. They hoped that the traders and the commercial gentlemen of the district would help them. He had been a little puzzled to know how to put the resolution into words which he had been asked to move. He thought the best he could do would be to put it in these words: I NOW DECLARE ON THE PART OF THE GREAT NORTHERN RAILWAY COMPANY, THE EXTENSION OF THE LEEN VALLEY RAILWAY UP TO PLEASLEY TO BE DULY OPEN. He had only one word more, and that was that the more traffic they put upon the new line the better would the company be pleased, and the more pleasant would be the remembrances of that day's gathering. (Applause)

"Success to the new line and the Great Northern Railway" was proposed by Mr. W. M. Oates JP, who remarked that they had now got in Sutton what they had wanted for many years, and that was opposition between two railway companies. (Hear, hear) The Great Northern Company was opening up a district which was exceedingly rich in minerals. In the Skegby district there were very large beds of clay, which he was told was of a high quality, and which would be found extremely useful in making high-class pottery, and he heartily wished success to the new line.

Mr. F. W. Fison MP responded and said that the Directors had not come there from any desire to do them (the people of Sutton) good, unless they got good themselves. (Laughter and cheers) Coal production was absolutely useless without coal distribution, and the company hoped, with the coal sidings at Kirkby and the sidings at Nebworth (sic), proposed under the Bill of this year, which had just passed the committee stage of the House of Commons, to get their coal to London, he would not say at a cheaper rate, but much quicker. Referring to the Great Central Railway Company he said he did not want to say anything about that Company. When they opened their line to London they (the Northern) would have a greater sense of freedom and less responsibility. If there were enough traffic for both, they would have it between them. If not, they (the people of Sutton) would, of course, give the Great Northern all they required. (Applause) Mr. Fison concluded with the remark, "YOU MAY FLIRT WITH THE MIDLAND, YOU MAY COQUET WITH THE GREAT CENTRAL, YOU MAY TOY WITH THE LANCASHIRE, DERBYSHIRE AND EAST COAST, AND WHEN YOU HAVE SOWN ALL YOUR COMMERCIAL WILD OATS, I HOPE YOU WILL ENTER INTO A LEGITIMATE AND LASTING ALLIANCE WITH THE GREAT NORTHERN COMPANY." (Laughter and cheers)

Sir Henry Oakley submitted the toast of "Success and prosperity to the trade of Sutton-in-Ashfield" and pointed out that he proposed it all the more willingly and seriously because it had been part of the aims of his life to extend the Great Northern Railway even to this fruitful, happy and prosperous district. (Applause) It was one of the greatest pleasures of his life that at the moment of his retirement he was there in person to see it realised. (Applause) The hope of the Great Northern Company was that Sutton might spread its boundaries, might enlarge its manufactories, might enlarge its mining, and might become the market centre of the district. (Applause) The company were in absolutely friendly alliance with the line which ran from east to west, and the charming Dukeries were within their reach. He could say much about their factories and the increase of their mining industries, but time would not permit. He was sure he expressed, as he did most heartily, not only his own feelings, but those of all connected with the Great Northern Railway, when he said he looked for the success of Sutton-in-Ashfield as one of the bright particular stars of the future.

Special trains were run from Kings Cross calling at Grantham then direct to Sutton-in-Ashfield via Gedling, and also from Nottingham arriving respectively at 12.15pm and 12.30p.m. After luncheon guests arriving by these trains departed about 3pm on a special working to Nottingham where they could take a conveyance "affording the guests an opportunity, if desired, of inspecting the works of the New Nottingham Central Passenger Station". This, of course, would be called Nottingham Victoria, when formally opened about two years later.

Contract No.2 related to the portion of line between Pleasley Colliery and Langwith Junction where the connection with the LDEC was made, and was under the supervision of Mr. Alexander Ross M.I.C.E., successor to the recently retired Richard Johnson. The contract was let to Mr. W. H. Hutchinson Assoc.M.I.C.E. of Mansfield who was assisted by Messrs H. W. Sadler and J. Lee, both qualified civil engineers. Despite being shorter in length than Contract No. 1 the cost of excavation and construction was greater, mainly due to the fact that much of its route required deep cuttings, one alone of 1 mile and 400 yards had an average depth of 42 feet and a maximum near to Shirebrook of 58 feet. Over 600,000 cubic yards of rock had to be removed which was achieved by going down from the surface in three stages, known as lifts. Furthermore stone of different densities were encountered, albeit only for short distances along the way which made the work more difficult. The top slice of the full width cutting of about five yards depth required Ruston and Proctors steam navvies to be deployed and gelignite was used, dropped into vertically drilled holes to blast open these rocks. The second lift involved driving a channel about 14 feet wide gradually sloping downwards from the surface, then blasting the rock on both sides of the channel, loading it by hand into skips pulled out by steam cranes. Once sufficiently advanced, temporary rails were laid along the sides of the excavated area enabling wagons to be drawn up to the cranes to facilitate loading. Work continued simultaneously at several points along the cutting and at times as many as eight steam cranes and eight locomotives were in daily use. The bottom lift was excavated in the same manner as the second, although as it got down to where the rails would be laid, its width obviously reduced. This work started on 12 January 1898 and took about thirty months to complete, much of the blasted rock being shifted forwards beyond the site of Shirebrook station in order to create embankments.

Shirebrook station with its adjacent yard was situate almost immediately to the north of the long cutting and here also was the junction of the three quarter mile branch line to the then new mine which was expected to raise 750,000 tons of coal to the surface within a few years of the line being completed. Here too was a rapidly expanding village of over four hundred dwellings by 1900, thus offering the prospect of passenger and parcels traffic to add grist to the mill.

Some 20 bridges were needed within Contract No.2 including the longest one on the entire Leen Valley extension, carrying Wood Lane over the railway in Shirebrook. The skew span was 81'4" and each main girder was 93'6" long, 8'6" deep and placed at centres 19' apart. Cross girders 2' deep and measuring 26'2" in length rested on the main supporting metals set 10' apart. Trough flooring was applied filled with concrete. The major bridges were all built to similar design including those which carried the line above roads. The company's official photographer has bequeathed for us photographs of every bridge between Kirkby South Junction and Langwith Junction, some of which are reproduced in this book.

Beyond Shirebrook station the line as built was carried high above the main road from Bolsover continuing on an embankment before turning slightly towards the north-west, passing under Langwith Road then on a more pronounced curve to join the LDEC at Langwith Junction. However the original plans deposited with the Bill show an alignment further to the west, the alignment being in a short tunnel below Langwith Junction station before making a connection with the LDEC Sheffield line prior to Langwith colliery, thus giving the GNR access to that mine. Later, after the line was opened there existed a proposal to make a short but steeply inclined south to east link to the LDEC crossing over the MR Mansfield to Worksop branch in the process. This curve was never built. Shirebrook station initially handled only goods traffic, passenger services being introduced here months later in November 1901. Coal trains using the connection with the LDEC at Langwith Junction commenced on 6 May 1901.

Bridge 10 carrying Stoneyford Road over the line at Sutton-in-Ashfield described as having "stone abutments, steel main, cross and longitudinal girders and trough flooring." The span is given as 27'9" square and 33'1" skew.

(GNR official photograph)

Bridge 2 on the south to east curve at Kirkby-in-Ashfield over a public footpath.

(GNR official photograph)

Taken from a footbridge above the GCR main line a little way south of Kirkby Bentinck (formerly Kirkby and Pinxton) station the northbound express goods likely to be making for York has Class V2 No. 60887 in charge. The last vehicle has emerged from the area known locally as "the Quarries", crossed the MR Pye Bridge line and is now on an embankment. Just visible to the right is the GCR empty wagon access dropping away to serve Bentinck Colliery. The lengthman's hut marks the approximate position of the long removed Kirkby North Junction at which point the formation of the north curve veered away left behind the third telegraph pole and out of sight towards East Kirkby Junction. *(David Dykes)*

This view of East Kirkby Junction was taken about 1905 as the lines veering to the left foreground towards Kirkby North Junction appear to still be in use although the points are set towards the South Junction. The public road overbridge is at the point where Victoria Road meets Lane End and is the main thoroughfare connecting East Kirkby (often called Kirkby Folly) and Kirkby-in-Ashfield, albeit both are now classed as the latter. The signal box became redundant when the north curve was taken out of use no later than 1908, but today Kirkby-in-Ashfield station on the Robin Hood line marks its location. *(Kirkby & District Conservation Society)*

DESCRIPTION OF ROUTE

The first section of line from the junction with the MS&L was especially difficult to construct, passing through a deep cutting carved out of very hard magnesian limestone to reach a point beyond Victoria Road adjacent to Kirkby's police station. Beyond this point, though still in a cutting, the line climbed to co-incide with the natural contour of the land close to the Butterley Company's Summit colliery where a signal box was provided controlling the two short branch lines leading respectively to the full and empty wagons sidings. Completion of the south to east curve was seriously delayed so the problem of serving Summit pit was solved by constructing a north facing junction between Victoria Road and the MS&L main line at Kirkby North Junction, the signal box there being opened in 1896. This curve enabled the MS&L to access Summit pit as well as allowing the GNR to take coal from there to Colwick Yards for sorting, despite having to reverse at the North Junction. The GNR erected a signal box known as East Kirkby Junction hard by Victoria Road, its location today being at the Nottingham end of the up platform of the present day Kirkby-in-Ashfield station on the Robin Hood line. No passenger station was provided for Kirkby by the GNR. Some two years were to pass before the south to east curve was ready for Board of Trade inspection, the signal box at Kirkby South Junction opening in April 1898, thus rendering the north curve redundant for the purposes of the GNR, though the MS&L used it for one daily mineral train for a few years till it was taken out of use in 1905 and then severed about ten years later when it was intersected by the Mansfield Railway alignment.

Summit box was of brick construction and provided with a 30 lever Saxby & Farmer frame. Sandwiched between the main running line and the two short branches on its eastern side it was opened as early as 1896 and continued to serve till about 1970. The highest point on the Leen Valley extension lines was soon reached close by the spoil heaps of Summit pit, then on a falling gradient of 1 in 120 the rails passed under the MR branch line from Sutton Junction to its terminus in the town. Still in a shallow cutting the rails passed below Station Road, then Outram Street to Sutton-in-Ashfield station, the largest on the line complete with substantial facilities for goods traffic to please the town's traders and manufacturers. Here to were a cattle dock and stable. The goods yard, used for many years by Gregory's coal merchants, also had a weighbridge. The entrance to the station on Outram Street where both ticket and parcels offices were located preceded covered stairways leading down to the two platforms each of which had two waiting rooms, one reserved for ladies, but both heated by coal fires. Locomotives could take on water from the cylindrical tank at the north end of the down platform, beyond which the rails passed under Priestsic Road to reach the signal box and sidings where the pick-up goods could run round its train. The GNR thought about making a short branch to Sutton Colliery as the signal box frame had sufficient spare capacity to allow for the necessary points and signals. A plan of the junction was drawn up but perhaps the cost of more excavations through the limestone made the Directors abandon the idea as the line was never built.

Proceeding in a generally northerly direction the next obstacle of Skegby cutting was encountered before the line reached more open landscape, crossing above the main Tibshelf to Mansfield road immediately before entering Skegby station. Here the alignment came into direct conflict with Buttery Lane at its junction with Mansfield Road causing the intersection to be moved to the west side of the railway. The previous intersection for the first few yards was rechristened as Station Yard where the entrance to Skegby station was at right angles to Mansfield Road. In contrast to the situation at Sutton-in-Ashfield the covered stairs from road level led up to the platforms, which, along with the waiting rooms were of timber construction. A small goods yard was located on the west side of the station area, but lacked a goods shed of any description. Access to the goods yard was controlled by Skegby Junction signal box located to the north of the station on the up side, and more importantly, the branch line to Teversal and Silverhill collieries went off at this point, climbing initially as it veered away from the main line. The layout at

The engineers have possession of the track for relaying purposes at Kirkby South Junction in this view looking south towards Annesley tunnel. The down GCR line is occupied by the engineer's wagons while Annesley shed has given Class N7 No. 69651 a rest from its customary duty on the Dido to help out with the work in progress. The engine stands on the down Leen Valley Extension line awaiting next orders while with so many railwaymen around you may suppose that the signalman's kettle will be in regular use. *(Frank Ashley)*

Now looking back from Lindleys Lane towards Kirkby South Junction the start of the deep cutting at the commencement of the Leen Valley Extension route is plainly seen as the line turns quite sharply in front of the signal box. In this view the layout is revealed in full so it is hardly surprising that several photographers came here in the 1950s and 1960s when the lines were busy. The Newport (Yorkshire) to Newport (South Wales) steel train has come via the Mansfield line, the junction being about half way down the length of the train which is headed by WD No. 90293. *(Author)*

One of Annesley shed's Class 9Fs has ventured at least as far as Summit colliery to collect another load of coal. The frozen snow has added a bit of unwelcome weight to the train but that will not trouble such a powerful engine and in any event the gradient is in its favour from this point onwards. Having no reputation for keeping its allocation clean this Annesley resident must remain anonymous.

(David Dykes)

As can be seen on the O.S. map there were several places in the Kirkby area where the lines of one railway company crossed above or beneath the tracks of another requiring the initial surveys of the later constructed lines to be carefully executed. Since the MR owned the earliest laid lines it fell to the engineers of the other companies so to arrange the gradients to allow sufficient headroom where their lines crossed over the Midland tracks, well-illustrated in this view of ex LMS Crab No. 42942 near the top of the climb from Pinxton to Kirkby (LMS) station as it passes below the Leen Valley Extension with a weekend excursion train probably from Matlock.

(Frank Ashley)

In the deep cutting beyond Kirkby South Junction ex LMS Black 5 No. 45368 (I think!) stands on the up line with loaded ballast wagons and is being passed by a down service comprised mainly of covered vans. Note the signal arms for both directions on the same post to allow for better sighting on account of the curvature of the line. Who said this line saw nothing but coal trains? *(Author collection)*

Emerging from the gloom and passing Summit signal box with about 300 tons of coal in tow is Brush Type 4 diesel (Class 47) actually in original two tone green livery though the locomotive is so dirty you would hardly know it. *(J. S. Hayes)*

"Summit Box" proclaims the nameboard on this brick signal box whose purpose was to control movements to and from the adjacent coal mine.   The base is slightly elevated to accommodate point and signal rodding visible adjacent and running parallel to the up main line.   After closure of East Kirkby Junction box Summit became the first cabin after leaving Kirkby South Junction. The signalman here has a good view of the running lines in both directions and from the top of the steps he could also see the points giving access to the colliery sidings which were on the opposite side of his workplace.

(J. S. Hancock)

A group of five local worthies (or is it four and the station porter?) seem pleased to get in on the act as the photographer stands at track level to secure the best view he can of Sutton-in-Ashfield station.   The result of his efforts was made available in the form of a postcard which was sold commercially in the early years of last century, perhaps explaining why several copies of this image have survived.   The view towards Nottingham shows the covered stairways leading up from the platforms to the booking office and station entrance fronting onto Outram Street. Note the up line somersault signal arm with white painted background to improve sighting and also the inclusion of Huthwaite on the nameboard, that village being about two miles distant. The houses on the left are on Park Street and they remain today.

(Author collection)

An unidentified WD 2-8-0 occupies the down line alongside the water tank. The signal has cleared for the engine to proceed towards the signal box just visible beyond Priestsic Road overbridge. The familiar outlines of Priestsic Road schools preside over the line at higher level. Reference to Huthwaite has now disappeared from the nameboard but for the time being the verandas on the platform buildings remain intact. *(D. Thompson)*

The shadow cast by the lamp decrees this to be a morning view of the station taken from the public footway adjacent to but separated from the railway land, and which links Outram Street with Priestsic Road. The nearer platform is the up side with the stairway from the station entrance creeping in on the left. The billboard proves this photograph is from the LNER period most likely before 1940 when some elderly carriages were still running about on the railways. The exGNR six wheel vehicles resting in the first road of the goods yard behind the down platform were used for the unadvertised workings known as "paddy trains" operated between Sutton-in-Ashfield and Teversal and Pleasley for the exclusive use of coal miners. *(N.E.Stead)*

Vehicle (and horse) access to the goods yard was from Outram Street. Once inside the first building on the right was this small brick affair shown on GNR plans as a weigh office. Its main use was for the distribution of house coal to a few merchants who served the town, but in later years it was effectively taken over by Gregory's Coal Merchants, the last firm to use it. The River Idle lies culverted below the road surface in the foreground.

(Gulliver collection)

The substantial brick goods shed in its final form had two external sidings on each side as well as two lines running inside from the opposite end to that shown here. In earlier days there may have been overhanging canopies on both sides of the building. The extension on the right is in different brick and is a later addition.

(Gulliver collection)

September 1954 sees Class K3 No. 61846 on excursion work. The destination is Skegness but to judge by the clothing worn by the two passengers it is not very warm. At least it is not raining yet! *(J.P.Wilson)*

Looking out from the window on the booking hall footbridge this is the high level view towards Skegby. Passengers have started to gather so a train must be expected soon, doubtless another excursion. A youth with his cycle has paused on the footpath to see what turns up. The veranda on the up platform building has now lost its glass, unlike the opposite one. Both buildings had general as well as ladies waiting rooms but the up side building was larger including a room for the porter and a small store, both under cover of the roof. *(H. B.Priestley)*

An unidentified and careworn Class B1 4-6-0 has called at Sutton-in-Ashfield to top up from the large cylindrical water tank, the only such facility on the Leen Valley Extension.

(Author collection)

PLEASE RETAIN THIS BILL FOR REFERENCE   A329/R(HD)

CHEAP TRIP
TO
CHESTER RHYL
COLWYN BAY
AND
LLANDUDNO
SUNDAY 15th JUNE 1958

| FROM | TIMES OF DEPARTURE | RETURN FARES Second Class to | | | |
		Chester	Rhyl	Colwyn Bay	Llandudno
	am	s d	s d	s d	s d
PLEASLEY East	9 30	14/-	18/3	19/6	20/6
SKEGBY	9 36	13/9	18/-	19/6	20/3
SUTTON-IN-ASHFIELD Town ...	9 41	13/9	18/-	19/6	20/3
HUCKNALL Central	9 56	13/6	17/9	19/3	20/-
BULWELL COMMON	10 3	12/6	16/9	18/-	18/9
BASFORD North	10 8	12/6	16/9	18/-	18/9
KIMBERLEY	10 16	12/3	16/6	17/9	18/9
AWSWORTH	10 22	12/3	16/6	17/9	18/9
ILKESTON North	10 27	11/9	16/3	17/6	18/6
WEST HALLAM	10 34	11/-	15/-	16/9	17/9
†DERBY Friargate	10 49	10/3	14/6	16/3	17/3
MICKLEOVER	10 56	10/-	14/3	15/6	17/-
ETWALL	11 5	9/6	13/9	15/-	16/6
		pm	pm	pm	pm
ARRIVAL TIMES		12 59	1 41	1 59	2 15
Passengers return same day at		9 1	8 16	7 58	7 40

(Due Etwall 11.15 pm, Mickleover 11.25 pm, Derby Friargate 11†34 pm, West Hallam 11.48 pm, Ilkeston North 11.57 pm, Awsworth 12.3 am, Kimberley 12.10 am, Basford North 12.19 am, Bulwell Common 12.25 am, Hucknall Central 12.33 am, Sutton-in-Ashfield Town 12.50 am, Skegby 12.56 am and Pleasley East 1.3 am).

†—DERBY CORPORATION 'buses will meet the return train on arrival at DERBY Friargate Station to convey passengers along the various routes within the Borough boundary. **Fares :** **Adults 9d., Children 4½d.** Passengers must obtain 'bus tickets at the time Rail tickets are obtained.

CHILDREN under three years of age, free ; three years and under fourteen, half-fares.

NOTICE AS TO CONDITIONS
These tickets are issued subject to the British Transport Commission's published Regulations and Conditions applicable to British Railways, exhibited at their stations or obtainable free of charge at Station Booking Offices. For LUGGAGE ALLOWANCES also see these Regulations and Conditions.

RAIL TICKETS CAN BE OBTAINED IN ADVANCE AT STATIONS AND OFFICIAL RAILWAY AGENTS
Further information will be supplied on application to Stations, Official Railway Agents, or to W. B. CARTER, District Commercial Manager, DERBY. Telephone: Derby 42442, Extn. 204 ; or NOTTINGHAM Victoria, Telephone: Nottingham 44381, Extn. 32.

Travel in Rail Comfort

May 1958   BR 35000

 LONDON MIDLAND   Arthur Gaunt & Sons (Printers) Ltd., Heanor, Derbyshire.

Three non-corridor coaches are more than enough for this local service to Nottingham, waiting in anticipation of passengers who are conspicuously absent, unless, of course, they are already on board. On a rather wet day the goods yard has signs of activity with wagons standing in numbers 1and 3 sidings. Someone has created a miniature garden on the down platform. *(Author collection)*

On a dreary and overcast day in 1963 it is nevertheless possible to see that the Sutton-in-Ashfield signalman is fully occupied with three trains to safeguard. A Woodford to Newport train comprising unladen bogie bolster wagons diverted away from the Mansfield line is adjacent to his signal box on the down line hauled by Class O4/8 No.63884 and is greeted by ex LMS Black 5 No. 45234 with a short goods working going the other way. Meanwhile Colwick shed's 4MT 2-6-0 No. 43160 is busy shunting some wagons originating at the Metal Box Co. factory at Oddicroft. *(Author)*

A similar view to the previous photograph but the cloud has lifted, the trains have gone, and the signalman is having a rest. If the proposed branch to Sutton Colliery (known as Brierley) had been constructed it would have left the main line at the far end of the sidings and curved to the left beyond the houses on Vere Avenue.

(H. B. Priestley)

A splendid view from Priestsic Road of Sutton-in-Ashfield station and goods yard. The latter may not appear very busy but at least five of the six sidings are occupied.

(H. B. Priestley)

Heading south partly shrouded in steam some of which interrupts the view of the I & R Morley hosiery factory on Penn Street Class B1 No. 61210 has a nine coach excursion destined for who knows where? The rear coaches are passing below the station booking hall and Outram Street on 30 March 1964. *(R. J. Buckley)*

The third coach is still on the crossover line thus confirming that this train starts from Sutton-in-Ashfield and, because the date is 1 May 1956, also confirming this to be the service introduced that year with the warning "use it or lose it" as explained in the text. With no passengers in view as Class A5 No. 69822 draws forward it bodes not well for the future. *(A.G.Cramp)*

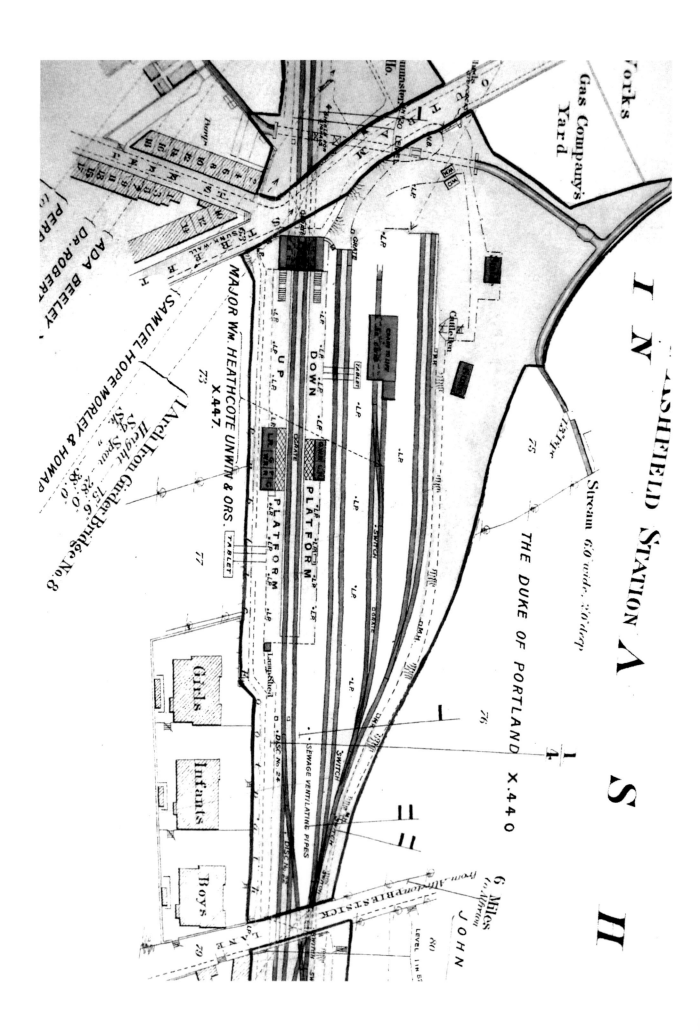

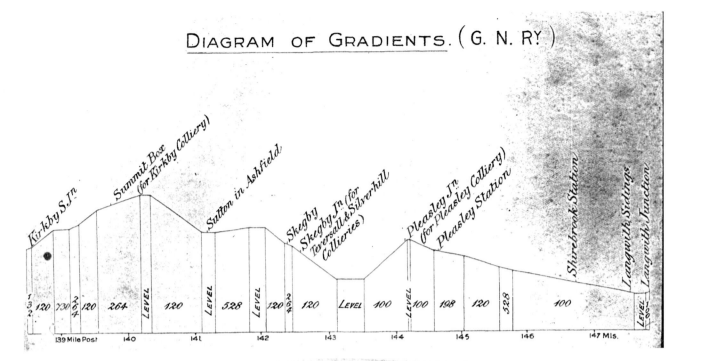

DIAGRAM OF GRADIENTS. (G. N. R?)

PLEASE RETAIN THIS BILL FOR REFERENCE   A17/R(HD)

F.A. CUP THIRD ROUND

NOTTS. COUNTY v. TRANMERE ROVERS
Kick-off 2.15 pm.

NOTTINGHAM FOREST v. GILLINGHAM
Kick-off 2.15 pm.

CHEAP TRIP

TO

NOTTINGHAM

SATURDAY 4th JANUARY 1958

FROM	TIMES OF DEPARTURE	RETURN FARES Second Class	ARRIVAL TIMES ON RETURN
	am	s d	pm
SHIREBROOK North	11 50	3/-	6 21
SHIREBROOK South	11 56	3/-	6 16
	pm		
PLEASLEY East	12 2	3/-	6 9
SKEGBY	12 8	2/9	6 3
SUTTON-IN-ASHFIELD Town	12 14	2/6	5 58
HUCKNALL Central	12 30	1/6*	5 42
BULWELL COMMON	12 37	9*	5 35
NOTTINGHAM Victoria ... ... arrive	pm 12 45	Passengers return same day at ...	pm 5 25
NOTTINGHAM London Road ... ,,	12 50	,, ,,	5 20

* SPECIAL DAY RETURN FARE—Passengers holding such tickets may travel outward and return by any train on day of issue.

SPECIAL NOTICE—In the event of the matches being cancelled or postponed, the special arrangements will be withdrawn and the tickets will not be issued, provided notice is received by the station of departure in time to cancel such special arrangements.

CHILDREN under three years of age, free ; three years and under fourteen, half-fares.

NOTICE AS TO CONDITIONS
These tickets are issued subject to the British Transport Commission's published Regulations and Conditions applicable to British Railways, exhibited at their stations or obtainable free of charge at Station Booking Offices. For LUGGAGE ALLOWANCES also see these Regulations and Conditions.

RAIL TICKETS CAN BE OBTAINED IN ADVANCE AT STATIONS AND OFFICIAL RAILWAY AGENTS

Further information will be supplied on application to Stations, Official Railway Agents, or to W. B. CARTER, District Commercial Manager, DERBY. Telephone : Derby 42442, Extn. 204 ; or NOTTINGHAM Victoria. Telephone: Nottingham 44381, Extn. 32.
E. R. WILLIAMS, District Passenger Manager, Farm Buildings, Granville Road, SHEFFIELD.
Telephone: Sheffield 29611 Extn. 25

Travel in Rail Comfort

December 1957   B.R. 35000

BRITISH RAILWAYS   Arthur Gaunt & Sons (Printers) Ltd., Heanor, Derbyshire.

Maroon London Midland Region station name and advertising boards look remarkably clean in this view of the public entrance to the station. Regrettably the photographer has not taken into account the height of the ornamental stone chimneys. The booking office window is behind the two ladies seemingly engaged in deep conversion but who risk getting knocked over if the next Mansfield District Transport service 101 bus is due. The billboard leaning against the wall offers trips to Skegness while a young boy dressed as you would in the mid-1950s prefers to study the furthest right one.

(Author collection)

Twenty years later the station is dilapidated but we can now see the chimneys. This view from Penn Street shows how the level of Outram Street was raised to accommodate the new railway necessitating provision of pedestrian steps and the protective railings.

(Author collection)

Skegby Junction was such that, should a loaded coal train out of control approach from the branch, it could be diverted into the goods sidings with a chance to come to rest before hitting the buffer stops.

The two mines on this line were deep and able to produce large outputs of coal which were taken away on the MR line towards Westhouses as well as along the GNR branch. Teversal was considered worthy of having a station as well as the inevitable station master's house. A single platform sufficed for this place which never carried an advertised passenger service, though it was used for miners' paddy trains running to and from Skegby or Sutton-in-Ashfield, as well as for private excursions, notably to the Lincolnshire coastal resorts for miners and their families.

Returning to Skegby Junction the main line continued downhill towards Pleasley but now carried for most of the distance on a substantial embankment formed from material taken out of the troublesome cuttings further south. The approach to Pleasley Colliery signal box was a short stretch of level track followed by a brief rise at 1 in 100 to the junction. Here on the west side of the line the Stanton Company had sunk its new mine, initially served from April 1897 by a single line from Skegby while the contractors had possession of the up line till October 1898 to facilitate construction works towards Shirebrook. The brick signal box was positioned in the apex between the main line and the colliery branch. The layout prevented empty wagons being taken into the colliery without a reversal, but loaded trains could get under way directly from the full sidings to the up main line where there was a brief opportunity for the driver to accelerate before meeting the start of the climb. Pleasley station, a short distance north of the coal mine, was in many ways similar in design and layout to Skegby, except that stone was used for the buildings instead of wood. All the stations on the line were entrusted to Messrs. Pattinsons, longstanding contractors to the GNR.

Building the line to the north of Pleasley was put out to separate tender as there was much heavy work to be undertaken in the Meden Valley between there and Shirebrook with no less than twenty bridges, some above roads being very high above the formation, and further deep limestone cuttings to be excavated with material thus obtained being carted forward and used to create embankments. After Pleasley Vale a stone viaduct carried the rails above a notable depression in the contours before Wood Lane. Two steam navvies and eight steam cranes were employed on this section of line At the northern end of the final cutting the single line branch to Shirebrook colliery went off on the up side just short of Shirebrook station. The branch, almost a mile long, fell away quite steeply sometimes on embankment passing through a residential area and crossing above Central Drive and Church Street in quick succession as it headed towards the mine. It was worked by train staff from Shirebrook signal box which was on the west side of the main running lines adjacent to the branch points. A refuge siding was provided on the down side. Shirebrook station was in identical style to Pleasley but neither of these places were provided with a goods shed.

The final section of the Leen Valley extension took the line at high level above the town with more embankments and bridges before the rails veered to the left prior to passing under Langwith Road on the approach to the LDEC at Langwith Junction East. Before that junction was reached Langwith Sidings signal box was passed, which controlled movements to and from two sidings on the down side as well as a refuge siding for traffic going south.

Kirkby South Junction was 138 miles 45 chains from Kings Cross; the distance to Langwith Junction East was 148 miles 8 chains, but in this line of just under ten miles (excluding the branches) the GNR had invested a great deal of capital and found the territory somewhat difficult to cross with a railway line. Nevertheless, despite taking six years to complete it must surely have been financially worthwhile particularly in the years before the First World War.

The entrance to Skegby station as shown in this view taken around 1900. It affords a clear understanding of the means of access to the platforms via covered stairways which included a ninety degree turn after the first few steps. The northbound entrance stairway is out of sight beyond the bridge which carries the line above the main Mansfield to Tibshelf road. A horse and dray loiters where Buttery Lane joins the main road. Given that the line and the station opened simultaneously one wonders why the stonework of the bridge support shows considerably more wear than the station building.

(Author collection)

Looking from the down platform towards Pleasley the signal box known as Skegby Junction is seen on the up side in the distance. The waiting facilities are of timber construction as also is part of the platform surface. Here the overhanging canopies have flat roofs with decorative fretwork similar to that used by Pattinsons elsewhere on the Great Northern system. The chimneys are quite plain, two stacks on the up side building denoting the presence of a porters room with a fire, unlike the down side premises which comprise only general and ladies waiting facilities.

(D. Thompson)

The pedestrian footbridge at 142 miles 27 chains from Kings Cross spanning the line at the north end of Skegby cutting shortly before the station is reached was 48'3" wide with steel lattice main and R.S.J. cross girders and concrete flooring. It remained in use till at least 2000, many years after the line was taken up. *(GNR official)*

This enlargement taken from the previous image shows Skegby station and the old houses in the vicinity. The outline of the gable roof of the stationmaster's house which remains today can just be made out to the left of the up line signal. The platforms were amply blessed with lighting provided by no less then eighteen lamps, four of which are visible on the up side. Note the position of the spectacle glasses on the down signal post arranged to aid sighting from an approaching train. *(GNR official)*

Ron Buckley has positioned himself on the previously mentioned footbridge to capture this high level view of Skegby station and its environs. The waiting train looks like an excursion judging by its length but as yet the engine cannot be identified. The staircase to the down platform is no longer covered, not so the other side. Buttery Lane is to the left of the station area, while the sighting of the down signal referred to in the previous photograph has been improved by the provision of a repeater arm.

(R. J. Buckley)

The train has now set off and the locomotive is ex LMS Crab 2-6-0 No. 42897 heading the 10.15am Pleasley to Dudley bank holiday trip on 2 August 1959.

(R. J. Buckley)

Skegby Junction signal box controlled the lines into the goods yard as well as the junction of the Teversal branch with the main line. Looking north the rails on the left lead to the goods yard which never boasted a goods shed, the main lines passing either side of the photographer. Beyond bridge 14 which astonishingly remains today the signal has been cleared for a train from the Pleasley direction but that for the branch naturally remains at caution. Some mineral wagons have been parked on the goods yard line safely away from the main lines. The signal box stands pressed against the shallow bank to its rear and its position can be ascertained today by the remains of a brick retaining wall.   *(H. B. Priestley)*

Looking south the two lines into Skegby goods yard remain in use in this 1960s photograph despite goods facilities having ended in 1952. Colwick shed has diagrammed Class 8F No. 48142 for the Silverhill colliery duty and while the Stanier engine is taking a breather Class O4/8 No. 63628 hurries by with bogie steel wagons making their way back to Scunthorpe. Skegby station is seen above the third wagon.   *(Author collection)*

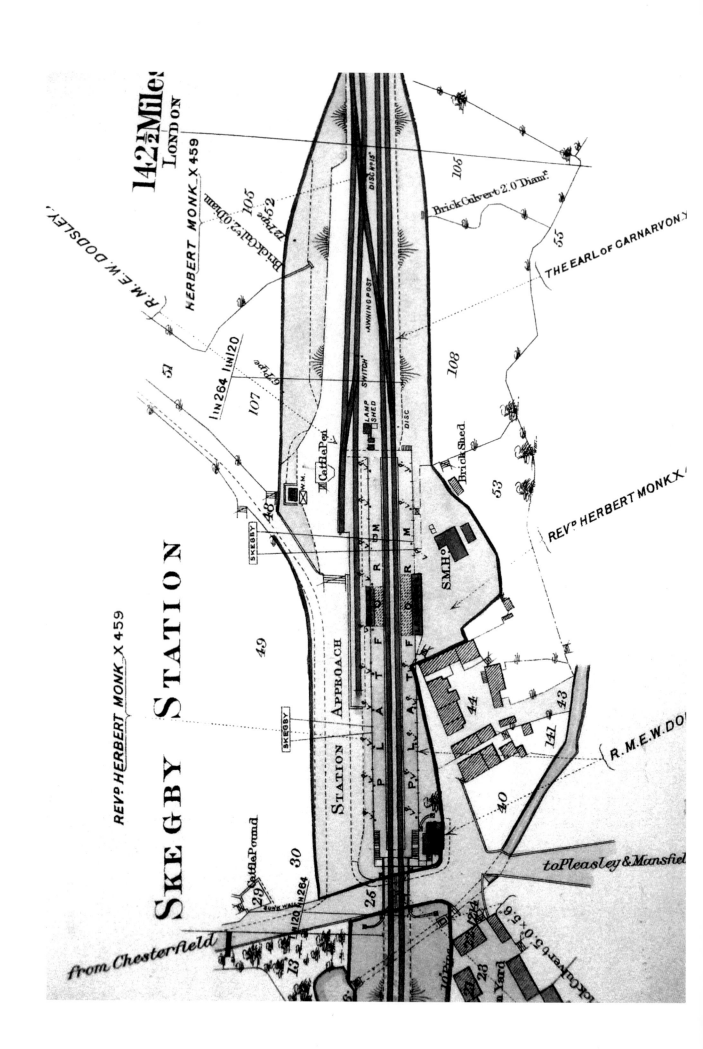

Skegby Junction showing the single line branch veering away left towards Silverhill and Teversal coal mines. A platelayer's cabin is partly obscured by the sign denoting a temporary speed limit of 15mph on the down main line. Not the usual fare, but interesting nevertheless, is the engineers' petrol wagon which seems to be undertaking a track gauging exercise. I wonder what will come along next? *(J. Cupit)*

Well who would have thought it? No need for much comment on this photograph, but I wonder if this item of national heritage will ever look like this again? One of its earliest outings in preservation the date is 18 April 1964. *(J. Cupit)*

It is unfortunate that the date of this delightful photograph of the station with some of the staff posed on the up platform is not known though it would be in the early years of operation. There are seven people on the track but who they are and why they are there is uncertain. Of those near the camera only two are known but four are wearing GNR on their headgear and it is interesting to observe that two of those have numbers on their lapels in the style of today's police officers. The older man standing is Harry Parsons who was a local farmer living on Silverhill Lane at Teversal. Skegby's first station master, Mr. Alder, sits with hands clasped. *(Author collection)*

Unusually clean WD No. 90000 rattles through the station, now renamed Skegby for Stanton Hill, with a short mixed goods train. The bracket signal for the Teversal branch can just be seen above the wagons.

(R. Morton collection)

Class O4/3 No. 63751 wheels another rake of empty mineral wagons through Skegby soon to be filled with the "black gold" which earned the line some money. The train has just negotiated Skegby cutting beyond the footbridge in the background.

(R. Morton collection)

A clear view of the station master's house is shown here standing tall behind the bungalows in what is now called Station Yard. The train is a Saturday working at 12.13pm to Nottingham Victoria headed on 2 July 1955 by Robinson GCR design 4-6-2T No. 69815.

(R.Cullup collection)

Photographs on the branch to Teversal and Silverhill collieries are quite rare but here a clean and named Class B1 No. 61250 A. Harold Bibby brings some equally clean (possibly new?) grey mineral wagons along the tree-lined branch.

(Author collection)

Teversal station which never had a public timetabled passenger service. It was, however, used as a platform for the miners' paddy trains which ran from Sutton-in-Ashfield many years ago, and also for the occasional special excursions put on for the benefit of miners and their families frequently taking them to one of the east coast resorts. Behind the station building, now converted to a dwelling, is the station master's house.   (R. W. Sheppard)

Class O4/8 No. 63898 has ventured up the branch to Silverhill colliery where it waits for next orders while the crew might have paid a visit to the nearby pit canteen to refill their billy cans. The 36C Scunthorpe shed plate might well be unreliable.   *(Author collection)*

The single line MR branch from Tibshelf Junction to Mansfield Woodhouse provides a convenient location from which this overall view of the GNR facilities at Teversal has been obtained. The spoil heap of Silverhill pit is prominent beyond the GNR station. The platform line continues beyond the guards van to service that mine which has produced some good sized lumps of coal visible in the wooden wagons awaiting collection by the colliery pilot. The lines going away to the right serve Teversal colliery passing above a public footpath which creeps under the railway in the foreground.

(D. Thompson)

LMS 2-6-2T No. 41320 has brought the RCTS railtour up the branch to Teversal station on 19 September 1959. The locomotive displays a 15A Kettering shed plate though it did find itself, along with classmate No. 41280, at Annesley at some point working the Dido. (R. J. Buckley)

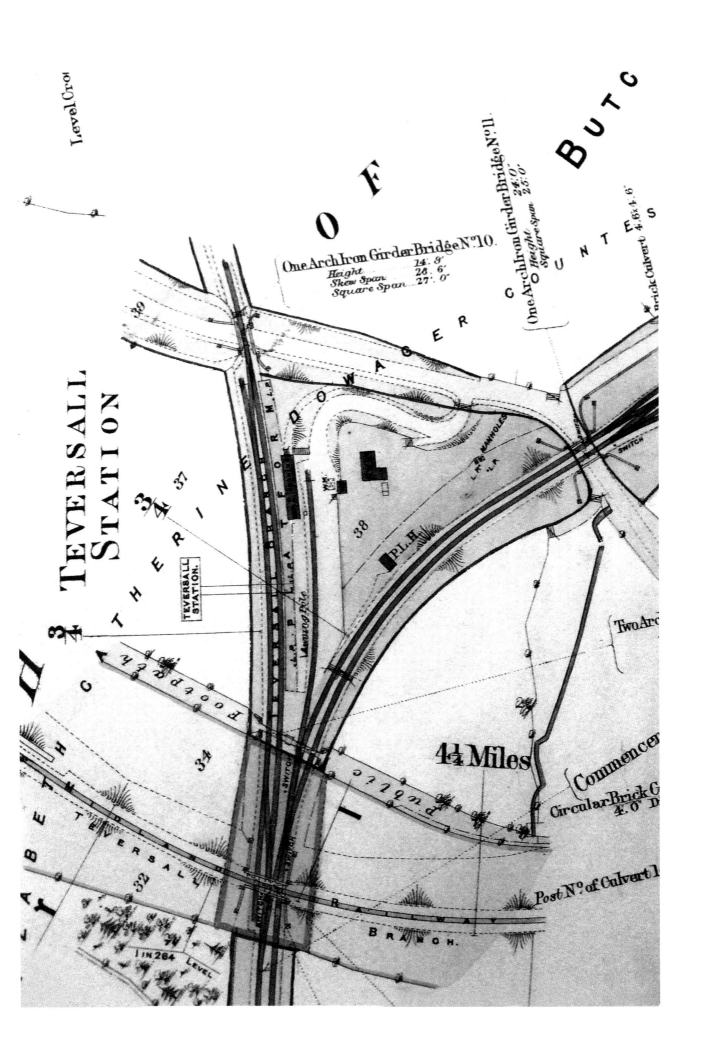

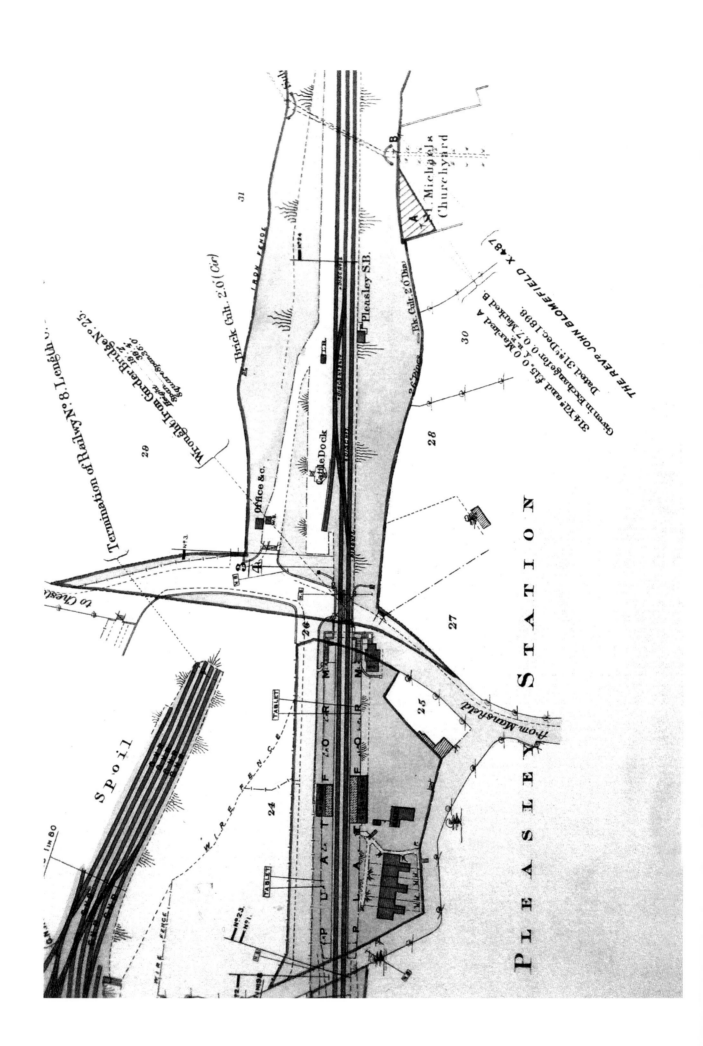

Pleasley Colliery Junction seen from the west side of the main line. *(H. B. Priestley)*

A further view of the same location but taken from the east side showing more of the lines leading to the colliery sidings where two roads are occupied by loaded wagons. The chimneys of the coal mine are in the distance beyond the signal box with the washery to the left of the sidings. The main line continues to the right shortly to reach Pleasley station. *(H. B. Priestley)*

Three views of Pleasley Colliery Junction, one of the signal box, one of four well-dressed gentlemen whose purpose there is something of a mystery, then one of four gentlemen properly dressed for the permanent way tasks at hand. *(Author collection)*

Pleasley station platforms looking towards Shirebrook.
(Milepost 92.5)

Class B1 No. 61405 at Pleasley in February1951 heading what may be a football special. *(R.J.Buckley)*

The start of the deep cutting north of Pleasley sees Class B1 No. 61302 passing through with RCTS enthusiasts special. *(Author collection)*

Shirebrook station has lost its canopies in this 1951 photograph despite retaining the signs denoting the ladies and general waiting rooms.

(D. Thompson)

Six corridor coaches should present no difficulty for a powerful three cylinder engine like Class K3 No. 61826 displaying express headlamps as it pauses for custom at Shirebrook.

(H.B.Priestley)

Bridge 36 over the road leading to Shirebrook station. The billboard headed Great Northern Railway advertises Nottingham and London as possible destinations. Does this image taken in 1901 show surplus stone in the foreground belonging to the contractor? *(GNR official)*

Bridge 2 on the single line branch to Shirebrook colliery crosses a main residential street in the town.

(GNR official)

On the same branch line the next bridge, of different style, takes the railway over a footpath. *(GNR official)*

Shirebrook station is hidden from view by the wooden hut as Class K3 No. 61981, tender stacked high with coal, moves an excursion on the next stage of its journey to Witton in April 1962.   The now trackless branch to Shirebrook colliery bends round to the right.   *(R.J.Buckley)*

Taken from the opposite side of the line another Class K3, this time No. 61960 sets off from Shirebrook but will only go to Nottingham, hence the ordinary passenger headcode. Taken ten years before the previous photograph the branch going away on the east side of the main line is clearly seen.   *(R.J.Buckley)*

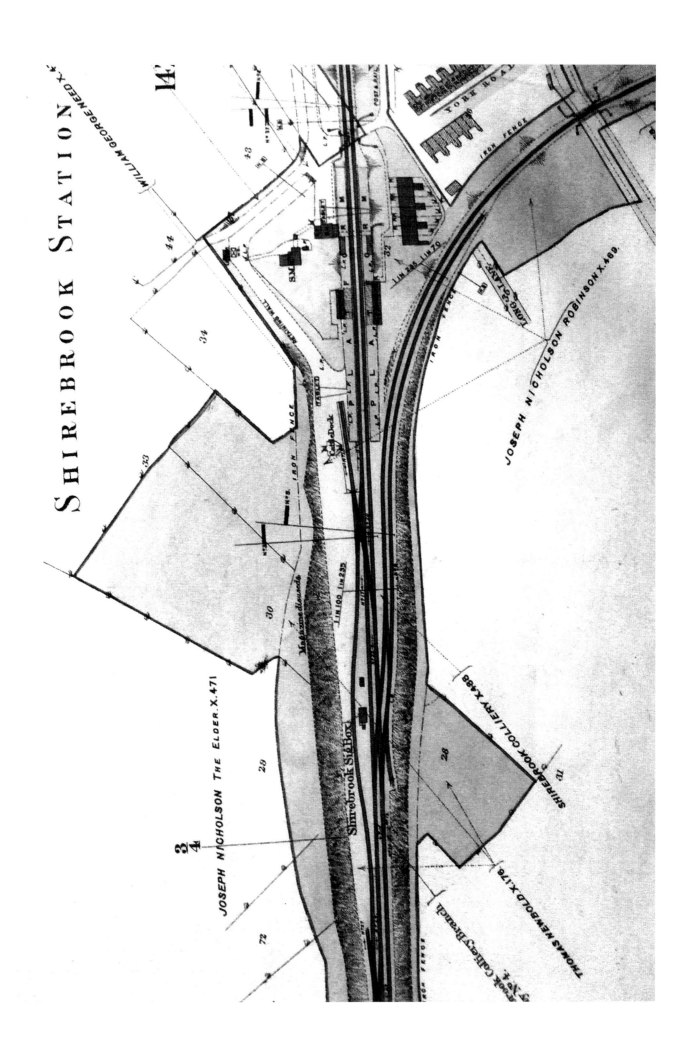

SHIREBROOK STATION

WILLIAM GEORGE NEED

JOSEPH NICHOLSON ROBINSON X.489.

JOSEPH NICHOLSON THE ELDER. X.471

Shirebrook Sig. Box

SHIREBROOK COLLIERY X.488.

THOMAS NEWBOLD X.176.

Now on the final section of the Leen Valley Extension Class B1 No. 61137 brings a Nottingham Victoria to Cleethorpes train high above the west side of Shirebrook and enters the curve towards Shirebrook North station, previously known as Langwith Junction. The date is 17 April 1960. *(R.J.Buckley)*

GCR design "Pom-pom" LNER Class J11 No. 64297 approaches Shirebrook North with a return excursion comprising six coaches which, in July 1953, still includes one clerestory roofed vehicle. The substantial embankments at this point are seen to advantage as the last coach passes high above the road. *(R.J.Buckley)*

This view on 4 May 1968 looking south from the Langwith Road overbridge finds a six car DMU (in fact two 3 car sets coupled together) on the approach to Langwith Junction, an elevated view from the opposite side of the line to the previous picture. *(J.S.Hancock)*

Still on Langwith Road but now looking the other way a short goods train hauled by Type 1 diesel D8198 has just taken the Leen Valley Extension route at Langwith Junction. The GNR provided a couple of exchange sidings and a signal box approximately where the timber hut stands all removed by the time this photograph was taken. *(J.S.Hancock)*

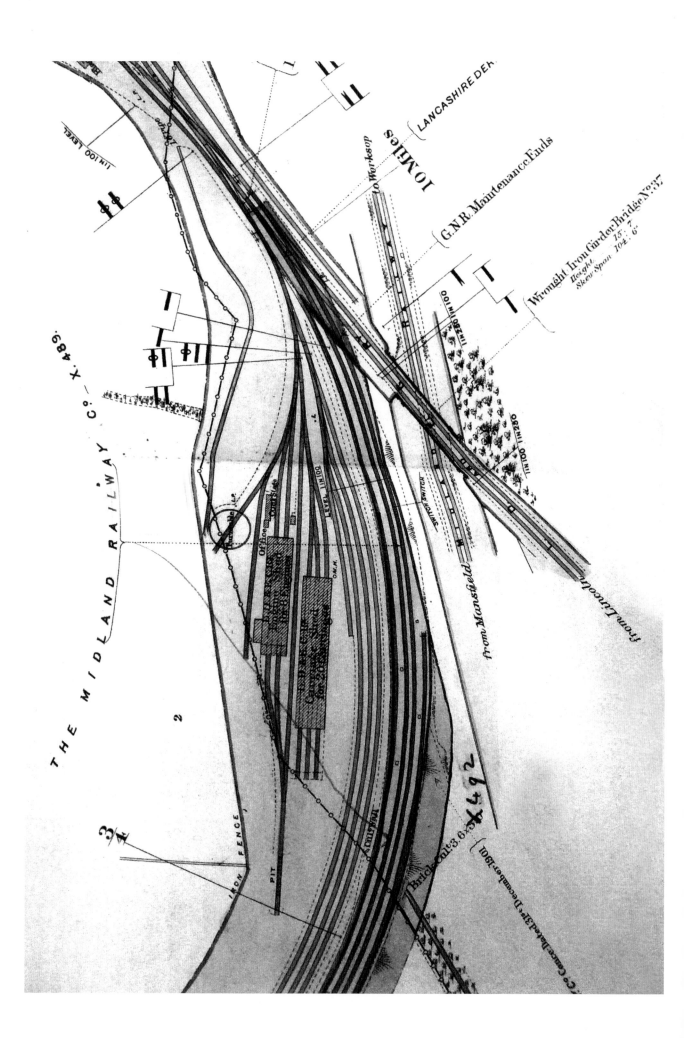

Approaching ever nearer to Shirebrook North station and with the concrete coaler and the tip of the shear legs at Langwith Junction shed in view, the last few yards of the Leen Valley Extension bends round alongside a row of the shed's allocation including two Class J11s. *(Author)*

The bracket signal at Langwith Junction shows the way clear for Class K3 No. 61889 to take the Leen Valley route on 9 June 1957. The excursion, whose rear coaches are still on the Sheffield Branch rails, is destined for Skegness via Basford. These locomotives were obviously popular with footplate crews for longer distance work.

(R.J.Buckley)

PASSENGER TRAINS

Although coal trains had been running to and from Teversal for some time via Kirkby North Junction it was clearly impractical to operate a passenger service in this manner. The direct south to east curve was inspected by the Board of Trade and approved for use on 1 April 1898 and the GNR lost no time in putting on a regular timetabled service for passengers four days later. The initial programme provided seven trains from the Nottingham terminus at London Road (Victoria was not yet built) to Skegby each weekday with one additional train on Saturdays. In the opposite direction only six trains are shown in the timetable, although two additional workings in each direction between Sutton-in-Ashfield and Nottingham appear. The Notts Free Press for August 1898 shows the first southbound departure at 8.10am from Skegby, the last of the day leaving at 8.30pm. Those calling at all stations along the route took around 55 minutes to complete the journey but three, including the already mentioned 8.10am ran fast and required only 40 minutes. On Sundays one morning and one evening train in each direction went only as far as Sutton-in-Ashfield. Motive power provided by Colwick shed was in the shape of Stirling 0-4-4T locomotives with their somewhat Spartan cabs. However they were strong enough to cope with the lightweight trains of the period.

The Leen Valley extension service was extended to Pleasley and Shirebrook with effect from 1 November 1901. The local timetable for July 1902 published by King & Bird of Mansfield reveals eight northbound trains on weekdays with one less in the up direction, as well as the same two Sunday workings which now operate to and from Shirebrook. However when Nottingham Victoria station opened its doors in 1900 three of the weekday trains ran direct via Carrington clipping several minutes off the journey, with the remainder still using the longer route via Daybrook and Thorneywood. This pattern continued with only minor variations till 1910 and probably until 1916 when the Nottingham Suburban Railway stations ceased to serve passengers. By 1922, now in the hands of Ivatt 0-6-2T engines, occasionally substituted by the handsome if not especially strong 4-4-2 tanks which became LNER Class C12 a reduced service of six down and five up trains were shown in Bradshaw, but two of these ran through the closed stations on the Suburban line purely to take in stops at Daybrook and Bulwell Forest. The advent of trams in Nottingham and motor buses elsewhere in the 1920s offering a more frequent and convenient means of travel to the public caused a significant reduction in railway ticket sales and the eventual withdrawal of the regular daily passenger service on the Leen Valley extension, the final trains running on 14 September 1931. Between 1929 and 1931, however, the LNER put on one train each day to Chesterfield (Market Place) by extending a down working to run beyond Shirebrook via Langwith Junction. This train frequently consisted of one of the Sentinel steam railcars, usually "Commerce" although "Rising Sun", also stationed at Colwick may have put in an appearance.

After 1931 the line remained in use and busy with ever increasing coal traffic, and the stations were left undisturbed and therefore available for excursion and summer holiday trains. Regular excursions had operated since pre-grouping days to coastal and other resorts as well as to both Nottingham and Sheffield for football supporters. The fares were cheap in order to attract enough patrons to fill eight or more coaches when car ownership was very much a luxury. Sunday school outings by train also appeared from time to time. The longer distance trips needed more powerful locomotives such as the various types of GNR 4-4-0 tender engines, the Class K2 moguls or the LNER Class J6 0-6-0 all perfectly capable of going to Skegness and back. From about 1924 the line was used as a diversionary route when the ex GCR main line between Sheffield and Annesley was either too busy or blocked on account of engineering work or a derailment, and in such cases the long distance express trains were routed away from the main line at Killamarsh proceeding via the Ex LDEC to Shirebrook North (the new name for Langwith Junction station) there to gain the Leen Valley extension metals. When this happened Sutton-in-Ashfield was treated to glimpses of expresses rushing by headed by Ex GCR Atlantics, the various Robinson 4-6-0 types and on rare occasions a Director. The latter type also appeared in BR days, but with the older pre-grouping types being withdrawn quickly after the end of World War Two, LNER Class K3s and B1s held sway until they in turn yielded to Brush Type 2 diesels in the final years of the line's operation.

NOTTINGHAM AND SKEGBY.—Great Northern.

WEEKDAYS.

	a.m.	a.m.	a.m.	a.m.	a.m.	p.m.	p.m.	p.m.	p.m.	p.m.	p.m.	p.m.		SUNDAYS
Nottingham ...dep.	5 30	8 30	9	9 40	11 15	12 55	2 45	4 43	6 5	7 5	8 40	10 10	...	
Netherfield	5 36	...	...	...	...	...	...	...	...	...	...	10 16		
Gedling	...	...	...	...	...	...	...	...	...	...	...	10 20		
Thorneywood		...	9 9	...	11 19	12 59	2 49	4 47	...	7 9	8 44	...		
St. Ann's Well ...	...	...	9 12	...	11 22	1 2	2 52	4 50	...	7 12	8 47	...		
Sherwood	...	...	9 15	...	11 25	1 5	2 55	4 53		7 15	8 50			
Daybrook	5 51	8 41	9 19	9 51	11 29	1 9	2 59	4 57	6 16	7 19	8 54	10 27		
Bulwell Forest ...	5 57	...	9 25	...	11 35	1 15	3 5	5 3	...	7 25				
Beestwood	6 0	...	9 28	...	11 38	1 18	3 8	5 6	...	7 28	9 1	10 34		
Butler's Hill	6 3	...	9 31	...	11 41	1 21	3 11	5 9	...	7 31	9 4	10 37		
Hucknall	6 6	8 50	9 34	10 0	11 44	1 24	3 14	5 12	6 25	7 34	9 7	10 40		
Linby	6 17	...	9 38	...	11 48	1 28	3 18	5 16	...	7 38	9 11	10 44		
Newstead	6 22	8 57	9 43	10 7	11 54	1 38	3 28	5 26	6 32	7 48	9 21	10 54		
Sutton-in-Ashfield ...	Stop	9 7	Stop	10 18	12 7	1 47	3 37	5 34	6 42	7 57	9 30	11 3		
Skegby ...arr.		9 10		10 21	12 10	1 50	3 40	Stop	6 45	8 0	Stop	11 6		

WEEKDAYS.

	a.m.	a.m.	a.m.	a.m.	a.m.	p.m.	p.m.	p.m.	p.m.	p.m.	p.m.	p.m.	p.m.	SUNDAYS
Skegby ... dep		...	8 10	...	10 15	12 20	...	2 2	4 10	...		5 45	...	
Sutton-in-Ashfield		...	8 15	...	10 20	12 25	...	2 7	4 15	...		5 53	...	
Newstead	7 15	...	8 23	9 55	...	12 33	...	2 15	4 23	4 45	5 0	5 57	...	
Linby	7 19	...	...	9 59	...	12 37	...	2 19	...	4 49	5 4	6 1	...	
Hucknall	7 22	...	8 29	10 3	10 33	12 41	...	2 23	4 33	4 53	5 8	6 4	...	
Butler's Hill	7 25	...	...	10 6	...	12 44	...	2 26	...	4 56	5 11	6 7	...	
Beestwood	7 28	...	...	10 9	...	12 47	...	2 29	...	4 59	5 14	6 10	...	
Bulwell Forest ...	7 31	...	...	10 12	...	12 50	...	2 32	...	5 4	5 19	...	...	
Daybrook	7 37	8 15	8 38	10 18	10 42	12 56	1 58	2 38	4 38	5 14	5 43	6 16	7 15	
Sherwood	...	8 18	...	10 21	...	12 59	2 1	2 41	...	5 17	...	6 19	7 18	
St. Ann's Well ...	...	8 21	...	10 24	...	1 2	2 4	2 44	...	5 20	...	6 22	7 21	
Thorneywood	...	8 25	8 46	10 28	10 51	1 6	2 8	2 48	4 46	5 24	5 50	6 26	7 25	
Gedling	7 44	...	...	...	...	...	...	...	...	...	5 57	...	...	
Netherfield	7 50	...	...	...	...	...	...	...	...	...	...	...	...	
Nottingham ...arr.	7 56	8 39	8 50	10 32	10 55	1 10	2 12	2 52	4 50	5 33	6 3	6 30	7 30	

It is 1910 and Freddie Gillford has provided us with this evocative picture of a Shirebrook train in one of the south bay platforms at Nottingham Victoria. Patrick Stirling's 0-4-4T No. 654 is nicely polished at the head of eight six-wheelers ready to leave on the circuitous route via Thorneywood, Daybrook, Bulwell Forest and Newstead, before reaching the Leen Valley extension. Observant readers may notice that this image of a local passenger train, typical of the late Edwardian period, has formed the basis of the painting reproduced on the front cover.

(F.Gillford)

An old postcard illustration from the years before the First World War shows a train from Nottingham soon after arriving at Shirebrook in the charge of another 0-4-4T, No.242. *(LOSA)*

Admittedly not of the best quality but so rare that surely this image of an express train diverted away from the GCR main line speeding through Sutton-in-Ashfield is worthy of inclusion. The photograph was taken about 1930 by Ernest Handley who worked as signalman there. He did his best with a basic box camera so we must not complain. *(E.Handley)*

Before then, in the 1950s BR was trying to save money by withdrawing regular daily services where it was deemed duplication existed on separate lines between two towns, and this included the Nottingham to Mansfield trains where both ex LMS and ex LNER lines appeared in the timetable. Plans were announced then notices posted in the local press proposing to discontinue the Nottingham Victoria to Mansfield Central train service but this provoked an outcry especially from the inhabitants of Sutton-in-Ashfield who had been used to catching their train at the former GCR premises on Station Road, reasonably close to the town. Now they would have to make their way to Sutton Junction on the ex LMS line over a mile away, obviously not as convenient and with a slower service to boot. Among the protestors was one H. B. Priestley, Head Master of the Brunts Grammar School in Mansfield, also an accomplished photographer of railways and trams. The number and determination of the protestors persuaded the Local Chambers of Trade and Trade Unions to voice their support for keeping the line open in addition to which three local authorities added their weight to the clamour. This concerted action failed to keep the Mansfield Central service going but BR did acknowledge that the people of Sutton-in-Ashfield had a point to make.

The Notts Free Press in its issue of 10th February 1956 reported that a petition signed by 6405 residents of the Sutton-in-Ashfield Urban District requesting the reopening of the station on the Northern Bridge was handed by the Council Chairman to Mr. W. B. Carter, District Commercial Manager of BR. Before midday Mr. Carter confirmed that the station would indeed be reopened to provide a weekday service of trains to Nottingham taking only 26 minutes to reach the city at a cost of two shillings and one penny return fare. With some reluctance BR agreed to run a number of trains between Nottingham Victoria and Sutton-in-Ashfield Town (i.e. the station on Outram Street) but gave warning on the promotional leaflet that people must "use it or you will lose it". Monday 20 February 1956 saw the first trains running but many ran at awkward times and people complained that the last train from Nottingham on Saturday evening was too early. The experiment was short lived, the final trains ran in October of that year, and the buses had won again.

In the final pre-grouping years and for a while in the LNER period ex-GNR 0-6-0s would be seen on the Leen Valley Extension. This photograph shows a typical passenger working although No. 35 is actually seen at Basford.
(J. Scott-Morgan)

TRAIN SERVICE

WEEKDAYS UNTIL FURTHER NOTICE

	am	SX am	SO am	WSO am	SX pm	SX pm	SO pm	SX pm
SUTTON-IN-ASHFIELD Town... depart	7 19	8 10	8 35	10 24	12 19	1 54	2 12	6 26
HUCKNALL Central ... ... ,,	7 32	8 23	8 48	10 37	12 32	2 7	2 25	6 39
NOTTINGHAM Victoria ... arrive	7 45	8 36	9 1	10 50	12 45	2 20	2 38	6 52

	am	am	WSO am	SX am	pm	SX pm	pm
NOTTINGHAM Victoria ... depart	6 25	7 15	9 25	11 25	1 15	5 44	10 25
HUCKNALL Central ... ... ,,	6 37	7 27	9 37	11 37	1 27	5 56	10 37
SUTTON-IN-ASHFIELD Town arrive	6 52	7 42	9 52	11 52	1 42	6 11	10 52

SO—Saturdays only.   SX—Saturdays excepted.   WSO—Wednesdays and Saturdays only.

NO SUNDAY SERVICE

SPECIAL CHEAP DAY RETURN TICKETS

AVAILABLE IN EACH DIRECTION
DAILY BY ANY TRAIN
ON DAY OF ISSUE ONLY

	SUTTON-IN-ASHFIELD Town	HUCKNALL Central
HUCKNALL CENTRAL -	1/6	—
NOTTINGHAM VICTORIA-	2/1	1/3

CHILDREN under three years of age, free ; three years and under fourteen, half-fares.

NOTICE AS TO CONDITIONS

These tickets are issued subject to the British Transport Commission's published Regulations and Conditions applicable to British Railways, exhibited at their stations or obtainable free of charge at Station Booking Offices. For LUGGAGE ALLOWANCES also see these Regulations and Conditions.

RAIL TICKETS CAN BE OBTAINED IN ADVANCE AT STATIONS AND OFFICIAL RAILWAY AGENTS

Further information will be supplied on application to Stations, Official Railway Agents, or to W. B. CARTER, District Commercial Manager, DERBY. Telephone: Derby 42442, Extn. 203; or NOTTINGHAM Victoria, Telephone: Nottingham 44381, Extn. 32.

February 1956

BRITISH RAILWAYS

B.R. 35001

ON AND FROM
MONDAY 20th FEBRUARY 1956

A

REGULAR PASSENGER TRAIN SERVICE

WILL OPERATE BETWEEN

SUTTON-IN-ASHFIELD TOWN

AND

NOTTINGHAM VICTORIA

Calling at Hucknall Central

THE CONTINUANCE OF THIS SERVICE DEPENDS ON YOUR PATRONAGE

USE IT
OR YOU WILL LOSE IT

FOR TRAIN SERVICE DETAILS AND FARES SEE OVERLEAF

Travel in Rail Comfort

BRITISH RAILWAYS

Arthur Gunn & Sons (Printers) Ltd. Heanor Derbyshire.

The temporary re-introduction of regular trains between Nottingham and Sutton-in-Ashfield brought a variety of locomotive types to the line. Here Class L1 No. 67760, a modern engine at the time, has been turned out by Colwick shed. *(Author collection)*

During the same period comes this view from a different angle of a much older locomotive of GCR parentage. The Class A5 No. 69822 nevertheless looks every bit as capable as the Thompson engine in the previous image. *(Author collection)*

GOODS AND MINERAL TRAINS

It was always the case that the capital expended by the GNR in constructing the Leen Valley extension line would be more than recouped in the volume of coal traffic originating along its route over a period of twenty years at the most, and this would doubtless have been the case had the First World War not intervened. Despite granting the LDEC access to all the mines served in exchange for access to Langwith colliery (and possible also Creswell) the overwhelming majority of coal trains went south behind GNR engines bound initially for Colwick yard, there to be sorted into trainloads for various destinations. As usual the LNWR secured running powers too, though in practice only operated a few trains. A large army of 0-6-0 goods locomotives of differing pedigree was stationed at Colwick GNR depot to serve the coalfield north and west of Nottingham as well as some 0-8-0 "Long Tom" engines and all these types put in appearances on the line.

The GNR had barely fifteen years revenue from the route before Britain's railways were placed under government control in 1914 for the duration. After the armistice the pre-grouping companies were to be compensated for wartime workings as if all years yielded revenue equivalent to that earned in 1913 but much additional traffic had been carried and maintenance suffered so the track and the locomotives were not in the best condition at the end of 1918, and nothing compensated for that.

The 1923 grouping put the GNR into the LNER system from January of that year alongside its competitor, the GCR, but one advantage of this, not immediately appreciated by the new management, was that four tracks now existed between Kirkby-in-Ashfield and Killamarsh under single control, namely the diversionary route referred to in the previous chapter as well as the GCR main line. From 1925 there were a number of occasions when the latter was so busy in the Staveley area that serious delays were caused to fast goods trains. The longer and steeper route via Langwith Junction was used as at least it kept the trains running. These express goods workings were usually in the hands of crews from Gorton, Sheffield, Leicester or Woodford, none of whom worked regularly this way so Langwith Junction was called on to furnish a driver with the requisite route knowledge, to act as pilotman. Apart from the odd occasion when a derailment blocked the GCR main line such diversions could be planned in advance and eventually they appeared in the working timetable ensuring that a pilotman would be on hand. The LNER was slow to instigate a programme of "learning the road" and even at Annesley and Sheffield, points to all intents and purposes at the two ends of the route, very few drivers signed the road via Shirebrook North until 1926. It was in that year that Driver Frisby of Langwith Junction shed was told to climb aboard an express goods which had been diverted via Clowne, and pilot the crew onwards to Annesley. He was surprised to discover that the steep climb from Killamarsh to Clowne, then the descent to Shirebrook North had been traversed by a driver with no knowledge of the route. Men from Langwith Junction knew the northerly part of this diversionary line whilst the southern section along the Leen Valley extension was worked exclusively by Langwith Junction and Colwick footplatemen.

From 1926 it became regular practice to send several of the night express goods trains away from the main line using a pilotman where necessary, though as far as Colwick drivers were concerned this only applied on the northern section of the route. The working timetable for July 1927 revealed nine up and seven down trains on week nights being diverted. All these were renowned for punctuality of running and the times of passing Kirkby South Junction are set out below:-

10.52pm   9.20pm Sheffield to Banbury. This was a Sheffield crew with a 4 cylinder Class B7 engine running non-stop to Leicester. The return working took the GCR main line.

11.00pm   6.50pm Deansgate to Colwick, which was a lodging turn shared by men from Colwick and Trafford Park sheds on alternate nights commencing with a Trafford Park crew on Mondays using a

Granted the quality of this photograph is lacking, yet this is a rare glimpse of an ex GNR tender engine doing a spell of shunting at Sutton-in-Ashfield. They had the nickname of "Long Tom" due to their 0-8-0 wheel arrangement. Does anyone have a better shot? *(E.Handley)*

More typical of the goods trains in pre-grouping years would be this view of an elderly 0-6-0 with a few wagons of mixed designs, such as No. 188 observed at Basford. *(J. Scott-Morgan)*

Class J6 0-6-0 until 1929 when former GCR Class B9s took over the duty. At the Colwick end the J6 engines gave way to the Glenalmond Class B8 type although occasionally a Class J11 appeared. Normally this train ran non-stop from Sheffield to Colwick but a seven minute stop at Spinkhill was allowed probably to give the preceding Banbury train sufficient headway as not all signal boxes remained open. This was not a heavy train and had the sharpest timing, 20 minutes, from Langwith Junction to passing Kirkby South Junction.

11.27pm.   7.50pm Manchester to Marylebone, another lodging turn shared by Leicester and Gorton sheds.   This train invariably had a Class B7 at the head.

11.40pm   7.20pm Stairfoot to Banbury which was in the hands of a Mexborough crew on their Class B5 4-6-0 also diagrammed to stop for four minutes at Spinkhill, probably for the same reason as set out above. The return working was via the GCR main line.

11.56pm   5.05pm Liverpool (Huskisson) to Kings Cross. Colwick and Trafford Park sheds shared this working on a lodging basis but the guards were based respectively at Deansgate and New England.

12.20am   11.30pm Colwick to Deansgate

12.48am   9.15pm Dewsnap to Marylebone. The diagram involved (in theory) a non-stop run from Sheffield to Leicester with a Gorton based Class B7 engine, but from 1928 this was a regular Class K3 diagram.

1.42am   12.10am Sheffield to Annesley, which was a more mundane affair, not really an express goods, but it brought the Annesley crew back to their home shed with their Class O4, or sometimes J11 engine.

2.12am   9.45pm Marylebone to Manchester

2.13am   9.30pm Deansgate to Colwick. The usual motive power was an ex GCR 4-6-0 of Class B8 or B9, but in later years the standard LNER Class J39 would be seen at the head.

2.49am   2.05am Colwick to Deansgate

3.02am   2.15am Colwick to Deansgate

3.13am   2.27am Colwick to Liverpool

4.31am   10.20pm Marylebone to Manchester

5.19am   11.22pm Deansgate to Colwick. The motive power here mirrored that of the earlier 9.30pm train.

The working timetable for September 1935 shows little change from that of 1927 in the up direction although the 4.56pm braked goods from Liverpool (Huskisson) went no further than Peterborough on Saturdays. Things were rather different going north with the 9.07pm Banbury to Stainforth fish empties passing Shirebrook North at 12.58am and a Colwick to Guide Bridge working extended to Deansgate going this way and finally a braked goods from Marylebone to Ardwick in addition to the other down trains already mentioned.   By May 1942 wartime conditions brought no less than eleven up and eight down fast goods trains using the Leen Valley extension between 10pm and 6am, a notable increase in the use of the line, and by this time the LNER was using more Class K3s on these workings.

LANGWITH JUNCTION AND KIRKBY (SOUTH JUNCTION).

Distance from Langwith Junction	UP. WEEK DAYS.		3	4	5	6	7	8	10	11		12	13	14	15	16	17	SUNDAYS 1	2	3
			7.50 p.m. Goods Trafford Park to Annesley SX.	10.30 p.m. Bkd. Goods Godley Annesley SX.	12.45 a.m. Coal Wath to Colwick.	3.25 a.m. Mineral Wath to Colwick.	1.15 a.m. Goods Deansgate to Colwick.	6.22 a.m. Coal Stairfoot to Colwick.	4.25 a.m. Empties Dewsnap to Colwick.	9.55 a.m. Mineral Wath to Colwick.	Summit arr. 7.18, dep. 7.19 p.m.	10.15 a.m. Goods Ashton Moss to Colwick.	6.20 p.m. Goods Deansgate to Colwick.	3.5 p.m. Petrol Helsby to Colwick.	7.30 p.m. Goods Dewsnap to Colwick.	3.5 p.m. Petrol Helsby to Colwick.	7.20 p.m. Goods Stairfoot to Banbury.	4.55 p.m. Braked Goods Huskisson to Peterboro' SO.		
	Class		A	No. 2	C	C	A	C	C	C		B	A	B	A	B	A	No. 2		
			MX	MX	MX	MO	MX					SK	SO	SX	SX	SO	SX			
M. C.			a.m.	a.m.	a.m.	a.m.	a.m.	a.m.	a.m.	p.m.		a.m.	p.m.	p.m.	p.m.	p.m.	p.m.	a.m.		
...	LANGWITH JUNCTION ... pass		1 36	2 51	3 26	6 10	8 30	10 10	11 11	1 30		6 27	10 27	10 39	10 57	11 23	11 53	12 13	...	...
1 4	Shirebrook South Junction pass		1 40	2 54	3 32	6 16	8 34	10 16	11 17	1 36		6 43	10 30	10 45	11 1	11 29	11 57	12 16	...	...
...	Sutton-in-Ashfield ... pass		...	...	...	B	...	...	...	B		...	...	...	...	...	...	...	...	...
9 37	Kirkby South Junction ... pass		2 4	3 16	4 15	7 16	9 18	10 44	11 48	2 19		7 37	10 50	11 15	11 30	12 0	12 19	12 45	...	...

KIRKBY (SOUTH JUNCTION) AND LANGWITH JUNCTION.

Distance from Kirkby South Junction.	DOWN. WEEK DAYS.	1	2	3	4	5	6	7	8	9	10	11	12	13	14	15	16	17
		11.15 p.m. Goods Colwick to Deansgate SX.	11.52 p.m. Empties Colwick to Wath SX.	1.25 a.m. Braked Goods Colwick to Sheffield.	1.50 a.m. Goods Colwick to Guide Bridge.	9.5 p.m. Braked Goods Marylebone to Mottram Yard SX.	8.30 p.m. Braked Goods King's Cross to Huskisson.	5.0 a.m. Braked Goods Colwick to Mottram Yd.	5.0 a.m. Empties Colwick to Wath.	2.56 p.m. Empty Tanks Colwick to Helsby.			10.35 p.m. Goods Colwick to Mottram Yard.	3.0 p.m. Braked Goods King's Cross to Deansgate.				
	Class	A	C	No. 2	B	No. 2	No. 2	No. 2	C	A			A	No. 2				
		MX	MX	MX	MO	MX	MX	MX	MO				SO	SX				
M. C.		a.m.	a.m.	a.m.	a.m.	a.m.	a.m.	a.m.	a.m.	p.m.			p.m.	p.m.				
...	Kirkby South Junction ... pass	12 2	12 39	2 9	2 50	4 36	5 10	5 50	6 14	4 7	...	...	11 25	11 35	...	...	...	...
8 53	Shirebrook South Junction ... pass	12 20	12 59	2 25	3 18	4 51	5 25	6 5	6 34	4 25	...	...	11 43	11 50	...	...	...	...
9 37	LANGWITH JUNCTION ... pass	12 24	1 5	2 28	3 24	4 54	5 28	6 8	6 42 B	4 29	...	...	11 46	11 53	...	...	...	...

(Column 5 marked SUSPENDED)

C56 WEEKDAYS — LANGWITH JN., SILVERHILL

UP		J	J		G		J	J	H	J	J		H	C
					EBV		To Stanton Jn.		5.24 pm from Stairfoot	9.20 pm from New Hucknall			6.20 pm from Dewsnap	7.55 pm from Ardwick East to East Goods
		3495	3339		3417		3497	3417	1265	3337	3299		675	715
		PM	PM		PM		PM	PM	PM	PM	PM		SO PM	SX PM
Langwith Jn. ... arr	1	..	..	..	..	..	..	..	..	..	..	..	..	..
... dep	2	..	..	..	6 30	..	..	..	8 51	..	..	..	10 13	..
Shirebrook South ...	3	..	..	..	6 34	..	..	..	8 55	..	..	..	10 17	..
Pleasley ...	4	..	..	..	6 40	..	7 5	..	..	..	..	..	..	..
Pleasley Colliery ... arr	5	..	..	..	..	..	..	..	..	..	..	..	..	..
... dep	6	..	..	..	..	..	..	..	..	..	..	..	..	..
Silverhill ...	7	..	..	..	..	..	..	..	..	..	..	..	..	..
Teversall ...	8	..	..	..	..	..	7 55	..	..	..	..	..	..	..
Skegby Jn. ...	9	..	..	..	..	..	..	..	..	..	..	..	..	..
Skegby ... arr	10	..	..	..	..	..	8 0	7 20	..	..	..	..	..	..
... dep	11	..	..	..	..	..	8 12	7 45	..	..	..	..	..	..
Sutton-in-Ashfield Town arr	12	..	..	..	..	..	..	..	..	..	..	..	..	..
... dep	13	4 30	..	..	..	..	..	..	..	..	..	..	..	..
Summit Collieries ... arr	14	5 9	..	..	..	..	..	8 5	..	..	..	..	..	..
... dep	15	6 13	..	..	..	..	..	8 40	..	..	..	..	..	..
Kirkby South Jn. ...	16	6 19	..	..	..	..	8 29	8 46	9 23	9 33	..	..	10 45	11 11
Annesley North Jn. ...	17	6 23	..	..	..	..	8 33	8 50	9 26	9 37	..	..	10 49	11 14
ANNESLEY ... arr	18	6 27	..	..	..	..	..	8 55	9 30	..	..	..	..	..
DOWN														
... dep	19	6 47	..	..	..	..	..	..	..	..	..	..	..	..
UP														
Annesley North Jn. ... arr	20	6 55	..	..	..	..	..	..	..	..	..	..	..	..
... dep	21	6 56	..	..	..	..	..	..	..	..	..	..	..	..
Annesley Colliery ...	22	..	..	..	..	..	..	..	..	..	..	..	..	..
Newstead Colly. Ety. Sdgs.	23	..	..	..	..	..	..	..	..	..	..	..	..	..

(Note under column 3495: Metal Box Factory Sidings arr. 4.38 pm, dep. 5.2 pm)

Following nationalisation of the railways in 1948 the number of goods workings reduced significantly so by the 1950s the line settled down to a staple diet of coal trains, returning empties, a daily pick up goods for such locally generated goods and parcels traffic as remained, but not forgetting the individual train dedicated to Metal Box Company output which collected wagons from the sidings adjacent to the Oddicroft factory between Summit colliery and Sutton-in-Ashfield, then took them to Sutton-in-Ashfield for shunting prior to departure around 6pm. Latterly this train was headed by an ex LMS Ivatt 2-6-0 inherited by Colwick shed following the closure of the former M&GN system. Coal trains were the preserve of 2-8-0 tender locomotives, mainly the ex GCR Robinson design either as built or as rebuilt to O4/7 or O4/8, supported by the WD Austerity design, whose numbers increased as time went by. Sometimes a B1 would appear when nothing more suitable could be found, but perhaps the rarest beast seen on the line was the ex LNWR "Duck Eight" 0-8-0 of Northampton shed. This would have worked to Colwick via Melton Mowbray and then "borrowed" before taking up its return working. In the final years the ex LMS Class 8Fs and Black 5s ousted the Robinson types, though the WDs soldiered on to the end of steam. The sight and sound of a grimy WD lurching from side to side and against all the odds remaining on the rails as is blasted up the gradient towards Skegby with a trainload of Pleasley slack is not to be forgotten.

In the final years of the line ordinary goods and mineral traffic, if not diesel powered, was more likely to be handled by 2-8-0 engines of different types. Indeed this region in the East Midlands has been referred to as "the land of the 2-8-0s".One such is WD No. 90340 observed near to Summit colliery.   *(D. Pearce collection)*

The houses front to Northern View, the appropriately named street on the north side of Priestsic Road. Sutton-in-Ashfield signal box sees the arrival of Type 2 diesel D7515 with a short goods train on 28 September 1966. Time is getting short for this piece of railway but all seems tidy and well maintained. *(M.Mensing)*

Brush Type 2 diesel D5821 brings a Sheffield Victoria to Nottingham Victoria local past Kirkby South Junction. The speed restriction of 30mph relates to the Leen Valley Extension going off right in front of the signal box.

(Author collection)

This train headed by Ivatt 4MT No. 43086 originated at Sutton-in-Ashfield but is seen just south of Annesley tunnel. This appears to be the usual formation of the Metal Box Company working which ran late afternoon and is likely to be carrying thousands of tins consigned to a factory at Melton Mowbray where they will be filled with pet food.

(Author collection)

Skegby cutting sees Brush Type 2 diesel D5817 heading a five coach train identified as a summer Saturday working from Skegness to Shirebrook North.

(Author collection)

6.WHAT IS LEFT OF THE LINE IN 2016

The 1960s was a decade of great change and rationalisation for Britain's railways. Steam propulsion was being phased out but not all the replacement diesels were up to the job, several classes of the new order having noticeably short lives. Many lines were duplicated none more so than those in the Leen Valley. Annesley shed which once housed thirty Class 9Fs and found work for all of them closed, further reducing the amount of traffic on the former Great Central main line which had already lost its expresses and stopping passenger trains. It no longer made sense to send out coal from the mines by two routes which had long since ceased to compete with each other over rates. Mansfield, reputedly, became the largest town in England without a passenger service from October 1964, when the Nottingham to Worksop steam operated trains were taken off, but there was no outcry loud enough to swiftly restore the trains, such as had happened in 1956 on the Leen Valley extension.

Generally speaking it was the former Midland Railway routes which survived along the border separating Nottinghamshire from Derbyshire. So with each coal mine having outlets to those metals, it was only a matter of time before the Leen Valley extension was deemed to be surplus to requirements. Goods facilities were gradually withdrawn during that decade and Colwick shed closed in December 1966, after which the line saw very little traffic save for the occasional special or excursion and the Metal Box daily working. Final closure took place on 27 May 1968 and the line went to sleep, steadily reverting back to nature. It had served its purpose......or had it?

Most of the track was taken up and station buildings were demolished, but the houses formerly occupied by station masters were sold by BR and they remain to this day. Constructed at the end of the Victorian era by Pattinsons to a standard design, some have been extended in recent years, particularly the one at Teversal, but the house at Sutton-in-Ashfield was extensively damaged by fire a few years ago, although the structure remains out of use. Additionally the station buildings at Teversal have been converted for use as a dwelling.

In 1972 the railways at Kirkby-in-Ashfield underwent a simple but significant remodelling which resulted in the elimination of a troublesome level crossing on the main road and a new alignment through what had been summit pit yard. The ex MR line from Pye Bridge was slewed to join the Leen Valley extension track bed just short of where East Kirkby Junction had been in 1900, the new route keeping to the alignment of the GNR line to a point just beyond the position of the former Summit signal box. At that point the old route was severed without appreciating that two barrier wagons remained adjacent to the former Metal Box siding. The marooned wagons had to be cut up on the spot, cut off by the new A38 road in one direction and Penny Emma Way in the other. The point where the line crossed the last named road on the level can easily be detected by two parallel lines without tarmac surface at right angles to the carriageway.

The portion of the 1972 diversion just identified carries passengers once more as it is part of the Robin Hood line, while the footbridge at the present Kirkby station stands exactly where the signal box at East Kirkby Junction once was. Then when work started on the second phase of the Robin Hood re-opening the alignment from Lindleys Lane to Kirkby station followed very closely but at a higher level the curve from Kirkby South Junction at the southern end of the Leen Valley extension. Finally you may still go through Skegby cutting on foot from Stoneyford Road to Buttery Lane, then either walk or cycle (or even ride on horseback) along the Teversal Branch and also along the main line as far as Pleasley, as these tracks form part of a network known as the Teversal and Pleasley trails.

Near to where Summit signal box used to stand the 1972 BR line curves away to the right leaving for former GNR line ending at buffer stops beyond the tree. Today the line is severed but a very short piece of rail lies abandoned close by the former junction at bottom right of this view.
(Author collection)

Typical station master's house more or less as built, this one being at Shirebrook.
(A.Henshaw)

After 1972 coal trains passing through Kirkby-in-Ashfield used the former GNR formation as seen here with Type 3 diesels 6826 and 6823 in the cutting by Harcourt Street, later to be the site of the Robin Hood line station.
(M.J.Hitchens collection)

The 1972 BR diversion at the southern end connected the former MR Pye Bridge line to the GNR metals close to where the points at East Kirkby Junction had been many years before. Two Type 1 diesels, D8022 and D8033, are seen on the BR alignment climbing the gradient on the approach to that location on 14 July 1972. The alignment of the long abandoned north curve is clearly shown on the right and the post and wire fence to the left marks the approximate alignment of the redundant MR line to Kirkby-in-Ashfield station which was built in 1892.

(M.J.Hitchens collection)

The 1972 diversion at the northern end retained a single line connection to the Oddicroft factory for a while, along the Leen Valley Extension, which ended in buffer stops just beyond the wagons in this view immediately beyond which the route was severed by the A38 Sutton-in-Ashfield by-pass road.   The single line also crossed Penny Emma Way at right angles.   The tracks shown here formed part of the sidings used by the Metal Box Company. When the connection with the BR line was cut it seems nobody appreciated that the two wagons were still there, so they had to be cut up on site.

(Author)

This view was taken during construction works for phase 2 of the Robin Hood line project where we see the formation of the new line on the right on the alignment of the original south to east curve but at a higher level, as well as the BR 1972 line from the Pye Bridge direction climbing to where the two will shortly form a junction. The footbridges form part of a public footpath in that area and both are still in place and well used. *(Author)*

The view from close by the present day Kirkby-in-Ashfield station shows the Robin Hood line curving away to the left towards Nottingham on the GNR alignment, and the 1972 diversion looking towards Pye Bridge passing under the footbridge. The former GNR north curve leaves the Pye Bridge line at the start of the curve and passes out of sight to the right of the bridge. *(Author)*